Leapfrogs

Athletic Activities

for Juniors

Jean O'Neill

A & C Black · London

First published 1996 by
A & C Black (Publishers) Ltd
35 Bedford Row, London WC1R 4JH

© 1996 Jean O'Neill

ISBN 0 7136 4138 X

A CIP catalogue record for this book
is available from the British Library.

Cover illustration by Eleanor King

Printed and bound in Great Britain by
Bell & Bain Limited, Thornliebank, Scotland

CONTENTS

INTRODUCTION

Primary teachers are specialists in teaching primary age children. Their expertise is such that they are able to provide a learning environment which enables pupils to respond positively and enthusiastically as they develop their abilities and personal and social qualities. As with all subjects, effective teaching in physical education (PE) combines this expertise with a knowledgeable use of material in seeking to promote learning through the maximisation of physical activity.

However, it is frequently the case that class teachers in the primary school have only experienced a minimal period of initial training in PE and may well feel ill-prepared to teach the National Curriculum (NC) Orders in the detail required; even though the post-Dearing curriculum (DFE 1995) represents a 'slimmed down' version of the original (DES 1992). Some of this insecurity derives from teaching a subject which involves the practical application of safety procedures: 'athletics' is usually perceived as being particularly constrained by such requirements.

As with the other titles in the *Leapfrogs* series, the content and style of this book are designed to assist primary teachers with the planning, delivery and recording of Athletic Activities in a no-nonsense approach which is cognisant of their expertise as well as their concerns.

Following an overview of what 'athletics' is, the second section will help teachers to align their knowledge and understanding of primary children with suitable athletics material in a way which will enable them to approach the teaching of Athletic Activities with fresh insights. Consequently, the following sections will provide staff with explicit guidance and many examples which relate to the planning and implementation of units of work and lesson plans within the early Key Stages (KSs). All examples are specifically relevant to the PE Attainment Target – plan, perform, evaluate.

The section on cross-curricular links and assessment strategies will help teachers to promote an effective transition between KSs 2 and 3.

Finally, the Appendix represents a quick reference section for the main points of athletics actions and techniques which feature in the lesson plans.

Acknowledgements

I am indebted to two friends, Lorraine (Flo) Playford and Margaret Page, both of whom are experienced specialist PE teachers. Lorraine is the Co-ordinator of PE (Years 1–6) at Ashford School in Kent, and Margaret heads the PE Department at Steyning Grammar School in West Sussex. I have great respect for their expertise and judgement. Both of them have been instrumental in the production of this book and I thank them for their support and encouragement.

...probably not what we have traditionally thought it was. Athletics is more than a multi-event sport; it's a far wider activity area which *eventually* leads to track and field 'events' as end products in secondary school. This broader perspective enables teachers to meet the requirements of the Athletic Activities NC Programme of Study (PoS) in both the learning approach and the content. The philosophy underpinning the NC clearly shows that the child is the most important factor. A pupil-centred approach helps us to present this area of the PE curriculum in an exciting, challenging way. The fundamental, foundation elements of secondary school athletics events are introduced during KSs 1 and 2.

It is also important to recognise the intrinsically competitive nature of athletics. Therefore, athletics experiences should not be presented as ends in themselves but as a means to an end, for a main aim of this kind of physical activity for *all* pupils is to provide answers to such questions as: 'How far can I jump? How high? How many bean-bags can I collect? How many laps can I do? How far can I throw?'

By implication, children also learn how to obtain such information by 'measuring' and recording results and in so doing, learn from an early age the importance of 'rules' and fair play, together with the accompanying acceptance of responsibility and respect for authority. As they move through primary school, therefore, children should be taught how to judge and record athletics performances.

The content of athletics moves through three main progressive stages: 'activities'; 'skills/actions'; 'events'. These stages can be related to the KSs of the PE NC which in turn derive from a knowledge of child development and the need for us to teach in accordance with their capabilities and inclinations. Therefore, by the end of KS4, the young person may be considered to be sufficiently informed and experienced to pursue excellence in athletics events and be able to: ...*prepare and monitor an exercise programme for a healthy lifestyle* (DFE 1995). The progression through these stages is summarised below.

		KS
Activities	Full, active involvement by all pupils. How well they perform is relatively unimportant.	1
Skills / actions	Specific kinds of whole body actions become more important as the purpose and response are closely related.	2
	Includes experience of specific ways of running (e.g. sprinting), jumping (e.g. for distance), and throwing (e.g. slinging).	3
Events	Certain actions are progressed to selected track and field events and simple techniques.	3
	Practice of more technically complex events, together with a theoretical input relating to biomechanical and physiological preparation for improved competitive performance.	4

It is of relevance to note that for too long secondary school athletics has been dominated by a teaching approach characterised by a preoccupation with 'events' and 'techniques'. This has led to a teacher-centred method of teaching in which the children are required to 'listen, watch and copy'. Strange indeed that this over-emphasis on technicalities has lingered on in athletics teaching, whereas other areas of the PE curriculum have been presented more in accordance with childrens' physical and social development.

By implication, therefore, distances over which children run, together with the weight and size of projectiles thrown, should be governed by a child's stage of development and not by the context of adult athletics events. The 100-metres, for example, is *not* a sprint for young children; they lack the strength and stamina to create and sustain powerful running. It is an event which is suited to older KS3 pupils and beyond. Younger children require experience of running fast over *short* distances of 30–75 metres, depending on their *age*.

A preponderance of event-centred teaching in secondary schools has also brought about insurmountable organisational problems: whole classes are required to 'wait for a turn' in long, high and triple jump events. Long queues and the consequent low level of activity for each child leads to 'boring' lessons with little or no opportunity to maximise their physical involvement.

Many secondary (and in some cases primary) teachers also rigidly include adult competition rules in athletics lessons. This unthinking acceptance of the 'traditional' has further constrained the development of childrens' expertise and prevented teachers from adapting and modifying material in accordance with pupils' needs.

For example, KS2 and younger KS3 children are usually asked to 'take off from the board' in long jump practice – a difficult skill which many international athletes experience problems with! If jumps were 'measured' from the point of take off, *all* children could achieve *long* jumps, rather than be discouraged by the teacher's loud pronunciation of 'No jump!'.

It is necessary, therefore, to perceive athletics rules as a means of gradually increasing the level of difficulty or challenge, and not as 'engravings on tablets of stone'.

The adoption of a pupil-centred approach in athletics teaching for KS1–3 pupils means that: (i) they are actively involved in the process of the lesson through exercising their decision-making and judgemental powers; and (ii) the lesson content is suited to their stage of physical and social development. It also implies that the teacher's role will *vary* between directing and facilitating tasks. Therefore, as pupils move through the four KSs, their experiences are such that they become increasingly responsible for their own learning.

Children love competing; they also want to succeed. The two are not necessarily incompatible, and through careful planning all teachers of Athletic Activities can encourage all pupils to strive to better their performances. This will inevitably involve them in different kinds of competitive challenge and a willingness on the part of teachers to adopt a broader, more realistic understanding as to what 'athletics' is. For many of us therein lies the challenge, for pupil-centred athletics contrast sharply with memories of our own schooldays. In the NC, athletics is... for the child.

ATHLETIC ACTIVITIES FOR JUNIORS

During the primary years, athletic activity experiences should aim to lay the foundation for skill development and enjoyment of competitive challenges. Some of this material, in KS1 particularly, will feature within the Games PoS and is reflected in the units of work and lesson plans detailed in the next section. It is this broad experiential base which enables secondary teachers to progress material through to selected events and associated techniques. As in PE generally, therefore, we should ensure that the content of lessons, and their presentation, is such that *all* pupils are encouraged to fulfil their potential and that progress is not seen to be limited to the physically gifted. Primary children strive to be active and enjoy competing; they relish a variety of challenges through which they can energetically seek to be successful – such attributes should excite any teacher of Athletic Activities.

This section, whilst focusing mainly on the teaching of juniors, also relates to KS1 children, as the transition between these two KSs is more a change of emphasis than a switch in material.

What should I teach?

The rate of physical development in primary children is high; there is a very wide difference in physical ability between a 5 year old and a child of 11. It is useful therefore to break this age span into three phases: 'the early years' (5–7, KS1); 'the middle years' (8–9, KS2); and 'the later years' (10–11, KS2). Clearly there will be overlap between these phases in terms of childrens' development and expertise; nevertheless they provide a useful guide in the planning of a progressive programme of Athletic Activities.

Early years (5–7 year olds, KS1)

These children should experience a wide variety of *activities* which are based on running, walking, jumping and throwing. The emphasis should be on tasks in which they work mainly as individuals, but should include an increased amount of pair-work by the age of 7 (and small group work by the age of 10). In this way children can experience simple competitive challenges involving tasks such as running towards different hoops and changing direction before each one, as well as simple combined activities. For example: 'Start on the line, run while carrying the ball, and throw it to land in the hoop.'

Older early years children enjoy competitive challenges involving tasks which they can complete as individuals, as well as other tasks for which they co-operate with a partner, or as part of a *small* 'team'. An example of the latter is groups of three trying to collect more bean-bags than the other teams in a given time limit. This task could be made more difficult (and in keeping with the 'planning' and 'performing' aspects in the NC Attainment Target for PE) if each team is required to 'work out' their 'best' way of collecting the bean-bags before starting the task. Can they beat their previous score? The greater physical challenge offered by combining activities for 7 year olds could also include working with a partner, or being part of a small team. For example: 'Take it in turns to run to the line, pick up the rope; skip five times on the spot and run back to the start.'

Middle years (8–9 year olds, KS2)

Running

Short sprinting practices (up to 30 metres) should contrast with longer runs (up to 150 metres) in which children should be allowed to find their most suitable pace – or, if they prefer, a variety of paces. The inclusion of 'trails', curving 'tracks' and 'slalom' ideas necessarily involve changes of direction and weight distribution, together with the speed variation required by the competitive challenges. Short (up to 30 metres per child) distances can also be used to introduce children to 'relays' and running over obstacles in the form of cones, skittles and canes. Other barriers may also be used provided they are low and will collapse safely if hit.

Jumping

Practices should include bounding, skipping, leaping, hopping and springing actions as well as jumping tasks, either as single skills practices or in combination, e.g. 'hop, hop, hop, jump, jump'. All this should occur within competitive challenges involving distance, time, height, accuracy and number.

Standing jumps, taking off from and landing on one or two feet, contrast with jumping after a *short* (i.e. 3 to 5 stride) approach. Sideways, backwards and speed jumping also encourage agility and control of the body weight. Jumping over various *low* barriers should include a *short* approach from different angles and may involve practising over a single barrier, or several successive barriers.

Throwing

Practice of various ways of throwing different kinds of projectiles enables children to learn appropriate ways of gripping and releasing objects, together with the need to 'anchor' the rest of the body during the throwing action.

Standing throws together with turning and running throws provide increasingly difficult but enjoyable challenges, all of which should include one- and two-handed throwing for distance and accuracy.

Later years (10–11 year olds, KS2)

Now that a broad foundation of athletic activities has been experienced, a move towards practising more specific actions/skills can begin, becoming ever more closely related to the event skills learned in secondary school.

Running

Experiences should be provided which give ample opportunity for children to practise running at different speeds over various 'circuits', 'tracks' and 'trails'. Sprinting for a set time (i.e. 4 seconds), or a set *short* distance (i.e. 50 metres) provides the framework for many competitive challenges. These include trying to 'beat' their previous result; trying to 'beat' a partner; working with a partner in competing against another pair. For example, pair A competes against pair B. Number 1 runner of each pair runs as far as possible until the teacher blows the whistle after 4 seconds; the number 2 runners start where their partner was when the whistle blew and also run for 4 seconds. Which pair ran further in 8 seconds? This kind of challenge could precede and/or follow tasks which focus on learning *how* to run fast.

Similarly, running over successive low 'hurdles' of canes and cones enables children to practise speedy clearance of obstacles, using a rhythmic running pattern in between each obstacle. Speed of reaction can be tested through fun practices of starting from various positions – lying down, standing on one leg, kneeling, etc.

Longer trails and routes around the school provide opportunities for children to contrast sprinting experiences with the need to pace themselves in order to complete these trails. Again, this activity ought not to be an end in itself but a means to an end. For example, team 'treasure hunting' competitions or 'word search' challenges provide great excitement and also require children to make some kind of plan together before beginning the task. Long and short distance relays are also highly motivating, although the use of batons is not necessary. 'Tails' can be hooked on to the next runner's shorts, or other ideas such as carrying and passing two tennis balls provide exciting team challenges.

Jumping

Children of this age increasingly enjoy trying to improve their performances in more specific jumping tasks involving jumping for height, distance and speed, with changes of direction and approach. Combination jumping requires greater co-ordination, is fun to do and allows for inventiveness on the part of the class.

Flexibility of teaching approach is essential. Canes and cones, together with knotted skipping ropes, provide the stimulus for various competitions which include standing jumps, different angles of approach, and successive jumping actions. These could also be structured through pair and small team competitions.

Throwing

With their increasing strength and co-ordination these children enjoy practising more specific throwing actions, such as overarm, slinging, pushing, underarm bowling and lobbing skills – with their non-dominant and dominant hands and two-handed throws. The kind of object thrown should be appropriate to the action being practised, i.e. quoits, foam discus, frisbee for slinging; tennis or rounders balls for overarm throwing, etc. Frisbee throwing is an excellent activity because of its unique throwing action, and it provides fun and exercise for the retrievers!

All throws may be practised from standing, as well as from varying types of approach. For example, the children should be taught *why* it is better to rotate before slinging a hoop than to run forwards at speed and sling.

Throwing competitions should include aiming or accuracy tasks, throwing for distance, and speed throwing, all of which may be combined with accuracy and/or distance challenges. Some competitive ideas are trying to better previous results, working with a partner to beat another pair, trying to 'beat the clock', and team competitions. An example of the latter might require each team to bowl bean-bags in an underarm throwing action to land in hoops placed several metres away. The further away the hoops, the more points they are worth. After a set time the team with the most points wins.

Before starting the task, the class could be asked to make up the rules for competition and to give, say, three reasons why they are required.

As the content moves from a broad foundation of basic activities and skills through to the refinement and practice of athletics actions by the beginning of KS3, so the teaching approach should reflect this trend.

All children need to be given the opportunity to practise, invent, work out, observe, describe and evaluate movements. Sometimes, for example, they can be asked to try out three different ways of throwing for accuracy, to select the 'best' way and also to give reasons as to why they chose it. Older juniors might work in a small team to devise their quickest way of running and collecting bean-bags, whilst trying to win the team competition in the process. A re-run of the task could follow a 'team talk' in which they could be asked to identify 'one good thing' about their performance and 'one thing which they need to change in order to do better next time'. After the second competition, did they improve or not? Why?

As an integral part of *all* of these athletics lessons children should learn to experience the responsibility intrinsic to a judge's role. In the early years programme plenty of opportunity should be given for children to 'mark' their jumps, for example. As they become more experienced in the middle and later years, they can learn to 'time' their partner's runs, to note where they took off from when jumping, to place a bean-bag where their hoop landed, etc. Later years children should also be encouraged to observe a partner and to give helpful advice about their results. This implies, of course, that the performer has to learn to listen to and use such advice.

This reciprocal learning style, which features much more strongly in secondary schools, could follow a teacher-directed task which involves a clear demonstration and explanation of, for example, leaping for distance. By allocating some of the responsibility for 'teaching' to the children, they learn to play a more active role in the learning process. This is essential if the PE NC Attainment Target of 'plan, perform and evaluate' is to be met.

Athletic Activities and Games programmes in primary schools complement each other through an emphasis on walking, running, jumping and throwing experiences. On the whole, therefore, the same facilities and equipment are used. Later years children, through being encouraged to progress towards more specific skills, *could* work in more specialist facilities such as a sand-pit or a running track, and use more complex equipment like stopwatches and tape measures. However, this is not necessary at primary level.

It is vital to use existing facilities to your advantage. Survey the outdoor area: to what extent is it possible to use man-made and/or natural features as, for example, 'markers' for a running trail? ('Run to the fence, turn left, and run fast until you reach the tree, then run slowly across the playground and back to the start.') Temporary markers such as plastic flags or cones could also be used to indicate changes of pace and/or direction, or changes of 'leader'.

A flat, straight or curved area would be suitable for teaching short, fast running challenges, fast starting and finishing, and running over obstacles – preferably on grass. None of these activities require permanent markings. A similar flat indoor or outdoor area may also be used as the location for jumping, springing, bounding and hopping activities. However, as children move towards the end of their primary years, their increased size and strength, together with their desire to become increasingly proficient in specific skills, requires the provision of soft landing areas such as mats, crash mats, or a sand-pit if they are jumping for height.

Throwing areas should, ideally, be flat and well away from other activities, pavements, windows and roads. Close proximity to a wall, wire netting, or fencing could be suitable for 'target practice' or other throwing for accuracy tasks. It is useful, although not necessary, if children have some opportunities to throw into a marked area to enable them to 'measure' their performances. Again, plastic flags and cones could be used to mark out 'boxes' or 'sections' of regular or irregular shapes and sizes.

Measurement of results could occur by awarding more points if the object landed in the furthest or smallest area. Children could also practise throwing at target flags or cones: teacher calls out 'Blue cone!', and the first team to hit one wins the challenge. Older primary children welcome the opportunity to estimate or measure at least some of their throws using a metric tape or by throwing into a previously marked area.

Distances in between the section lines could be measured accurately by using lengths of wood (or pieces of old tape), marked in centimetres. In this way children could experience different ways of throwing various objects whilst taking part in, for example, a team competition.

Much commercially produced athletics equipment is expensive and/or inappropriate in both weight and size, and unnecessary for primary Athletic Activities. Games equipment is ideal, and teachers should be open-minded, inventive and flexible in its use.

The following information underpins all areas of activity in the PE NC and applies across all KSs. They are general requirements.

(1) To promote physical activity and healthy lifestyles, pupils should be taught:

(a) to be physically active
(b) to adopt the best possible posture and the appropriate use of the body
(c) to engage in activities that develop cardiovascular health, flexibility, muscular strength and endurance
(d) the increasing need for personal hygiene in relation to vigorous physical activity.

(2) To develop positive attitudes, pupils should be taught:

(a) to observe the conventions of fair play, honest competition and good sporting behaviour as individual participants, team members and spectators
(b) how to cope with success and limitations in performance
(c) to try hard to consolidate their performances
(d) to be mindful of others and the environment.

(3) To ensure safe practice, pupils should be taught:

(a) to respond readily to instructions
(b) to recognise and follow relevant rules, laws, codes, etiquette and safety procedures for different activities or events, in practice and during competition
(c) about the safety risks of wearing inappropriate clothing, footwear and jewellery and why particular clothing, footwear and protection are worn for different activities
(d) how to lift, carry, place and use equipment safely
(e) to warm up for and recover from exercise.

In addition, the PE NC's End of KS1 Description states that the majority of pupils should:

…plan and perform simple skills safely and show control in linking actions together. They improve their performance through practising their skills, working alone and with a partner. They talk about what they and others have done and are able to make simple judgements. They recognise and describe the changes that happen to their bodies during exercise. (DFE 1995:11)

There are three mandatory activity areas in KS1: Gymnastic Activities, Dance and Games (DFE 1995). The previous sections of this book have emphasised the similarities between Athletic Activities and Games, particularly in KS1. This is borne out in two of the three PoS statements in the Games activity area:

Pupils should be taught: (b) to develop and practise a variety of ways of sending (including throwing … rolling and bouncing) … (c) elements of games play that include running, chasing, dodging, avoiding and awareness of space and other players. (op cit:3)

To summarise, in KS1 Athletic Activities there are three main categories of content: running, jumping and throwing. Each category may be sub-divided into main areas of emphasis from which units of work and lesson plans are devised.

Running: (for) variety, speed and distance.
Jumping: (for) variety, speed, distance, height, accuracy, travel.
Throwing: (for) variety, speed, distance, height, accuracy.

The following lesson plans give clear, concise ideas for teaching these walking, running, jumping and throwing activities to KS1 children, and in so doing enable progression of content to occur within and between lessons and throughout the KS. In PE we should always aim to promote pupils' cardiovascular fitness: therefore running features in every lesson throughout the KS.

Each lesson has the following structure.

Warming: 5 minutes.
Running activity: 10 minutes.
Main activities: 15 minutes.
Concluding activity: 5 minutes.

The warming represents a *gradual* introduction to exercise, through which the body temperature is raised, prior to gentle stretching exercises which aim to increase pupils' mobility and flexibility, thereby preparing the body to perform at maximal speed and range of movement. Therefore, start with some gentle jogging, skipping, or brisk walking tasks, during which pupils move *constantly*. This is followed by stretching exercises, all carried out slowly, without jerking or straining, for example:

(a) move head from front facing to side; side to front; front to other side, x5
(b) raise shoulders slowly; together x5, then one shoulder x5, then the other x5
(c) circle arms slowly backwards x5, then forwards x5; one arm circles x5, then the other arm x5
(d) lift arms out to the side of the body and rotate them inwards/outwards x5
(e) stand astride, feet shoulder width apart; turn the upper part of the body as far as it will go then return to be front facing; repeat rotating to the other side, x5
(f) bend over until the fingers/hands touch the ground and the arms dangle; stretch up to reach as far as possible then repeat x5
(g) stand with legs slightly bent, feet together; slowly reach down to touch the ground then stand up again, x5.

The concluding activity serves to calm the pupils down, both physically and mentally, before they return to the classroom. Obviously, these final tasks must be carried out slowly and as a whole class activity. Examples include:

(a) standing, rise up on to the toes x3 and walk away with good posture
(b) lying on the back with all limbs in a naturally straight position, arms by the sides; gradually stand and go through (a) above
(c) jogging slowly on the spot, decrease speed and movement until standing still; do (a) above.

There follows a complete unit of work for each year of the KS (12 lessons per year). Progression of difficulty occurs within and between years and between KS1 and 2. Whilst all the tasks included in these plans have been taught to juniors, the author recognises that variation exists in the capabilities and aptitudes between pupils of the same age in different schools, and that the schools themselves possess various types and amount of equipment and differing facilities. It is important, therefore, that teaching staff use and, if necessary, modify these lessons to suit their situation and their childrens' needs.

KEY STAGE 1
LESSON PLANS

Key Stage 1 • Year 1 • Lesson 1

LEARNING OUTCOMES

1 To vary the speed of walking.
2 To combine hopping and jumping activities.

Section	Content	Points	Facilities / equipment
Warm-up			
Main activity or challenge	**Walking**		
	1 Walk avoiding others.	Awareness of space and others.	Large defined area marked out with either lines or cones.
	2 Walk slowly then quickly.	Use of whistle.	
	3 Teach fast walking.	Short steps and fast arm movements. Heel of 1 foot and toe of other must be grounded.	
	4 Walk again with change of speed.	Use of whistle.	
	5 Walking races in small groups over short distances (15/20m).	Demonstrate walking action.	Lines/markers to be used for start and finish, no lanes.
	Jumping		
	1 Hop on spot; 3 on one foot then 3 on other foot.	Head up, and use of arms for balance.	In a space.
	2 Hop forwards; then backwards and sideways.	Head up, and use of arms for balance.	
	3 Hop-hop-jump, then repeat.	Rhythm. Land on two feet when jumping.	
	4 Practice hopping for distance. Competition in 2's.	Push hard. Bend ankles/ knees when landing. Demonstration. 3 turns each. 1 hops and 1 marks. Measure to back of heel.	In a space; take-off line/mark, 2 markers/ couple.
	5 In 2's, there-and-back hopping relay over a short distance (10m).	Must touch next person before that person can start. Must go round marker.	Lines/markers to be used for start and return.
Concluding activity			

Key Stage 1 • Year 1 • Lesson 2

LEARNING OUTCOMES

1 To walk with speed and direction changes.
2 To hop in different directions.

Section	Content	Points	Facilities / equipment
Warm-up			
Main activity or challenge	**Walking**		
	1 Revise walking with change of speed.	Revise action from week 1. Use of whistle.	Large defined area marked out with lines or cones.
	2 Walk changing direction: forwards, backwards, sideways.	Look behind when walking backwards. Small steps to change direction.	
	3 Start at a cone. Walk and change direction at each cone.	Awareness of others and cones.	Cones scattered in large defined area.
	4 Start at a cone. Walk and change speed at each one.		
	Jumping		
	1 Revise hopping forwards, backwards, sideways.	Develop to use a combination, e.g. forwards and backwards, side to side.	Ropes/hoops could be used, in a space.
	2 Hop for height.	Push hard. Bend knee/ ankle when landing.	In a space.
	3 Fours practice hopping for height. Competition in fours.	Experiment: hop forwards, backwards, sideways. Which way is best? Demonstration.	Low obstacles such as skittles and canes, in a space.
	4 Hopping circuit for distance, variety, height.	All go round the same way. Demonstration.	Skittles and canes of varying heights; 2 ropes at varying distances apart; hoops; cones; bean bags, etc.
Concluding activity			

LEARNING OUTCOMES

1 To combine walking and running actions.
2 To practice the 2-handed-push throwing action.
3 To take part in a 20m walking/running race.

Section	Content	Points	Facilities / equipment
Warm-up			
Main activity or challenge	**Walking and running**		
	1 Revise walk with change of speed.	Use a whistle. Awareness of space and others.	Large defined area marked out with lines/cones.
	2 Run avoiding others.	Awareness of space and others.	
	3 Teach running.	Run on balls of feet (try it on heels for contrast), with elbows in. Demonstration.	
	4 Fast walk then run, fast walk then run.	Awareness of space, others, change of speed.	
	Throwing		
	1 In 2's throw ball to partner. Throw or catch in these positions: a) sitting, b) kneeling, c) standing.	Correct pushing action. Demonstration.	Class forms 2 lines in a space, 2m apart facing each other and on line/ marker.
	2 In 2's throw ball to partner 3 times, then both take 1 step back, etc. If ball is dropped, then 1 step is taken forwards by both.	Winning couple are those furthest away from each other after a set time.	
	Walking and running		
	Walking and running race. Line children up. Race over 20m. Person nearest finish line/mark at the final whistle is the winner.	Use of whistle to alternate between walking and running.	Lines/markers to be used for start and finish; no lanes.
Concluding activity			

Key Stage 1 • Year 1 • Lesson 4

LEARNING OUTCOMES

1 To walk and run in races.
2 To practice the 2-handed-push throwing action.
3 To take part in a running relay.

Section	Content	Points	Facilities / equipment
Warm-up			
Main activity or challenge	**Walking and running**		
	1 Walk-run-walk from cone to cone.	Awareness of change of speed.	3 cones per child, 6m apart; each set of cones 2m apart; lines/markers to be used for start.
	2 Walk forwards to cone 1, backwards to cone 2, sideways to cone 3.	Small steps to change direction. Look behind when walking backwards.	
	3 Repeat No.2 but running.	Demonstration.	
	4 Repeat No.3 as a race.		
	Throwing: 2-handed push		
	1 In 2's, 1 throws to target while a) sitting, b) kneeling, c) standing, then other retrieves. 3 throws in each position, then change over.	Revise technique by Q/A session: fingers spread, elbows out – follow through. 1 foot in front of other when standing. Push action demonstration.	In a space or on a line/marker for throwing point; hoop for target; quoit/ball for throwing; hoop 3m from throwing line.
	2 Competition in 2's.	Competition for aiming/accuracy. Who gained the most points?	3 hoops suitably spaced out; line/marker for throwing point; 3 balls/quoits.
	3 3 throws each from standing. Whole or part of ball/quoit must land in hoop: 1 point for 1st hoop, etc.		
	Running relay		
	In 3's there-and-back running relay over short distance (10m). No.1 runs forwards, No.2 runs backwards, No.3 runs sideways. Run to marker and back.	Must touch next person before that person goes.	Line/markers to be used for start and return.
Concluding activity			

LEARNING OUTCOMES

1 To walk/run on 'tracks'.
2 To bounce for distance and in different directions.

Section	Content	Points	Facilities / equipment
Warm-up			
Main activity or challenge	***Walking and running***		
	1 Revise walk-run-walk.	Awareness of space, others and change of speed.	Large defined area marked out with lines or cones.
	2 Walk quickly, using different tracks. Travel from 1 marker to the other.	Look for variety: straight, curved, zig-zag, etc. Demonstration.	2 markers per child, 10m apart; each set of markers 2m apart.
	3 All walk from 1 marker to the other, using the three different tracks.	Small steps when changing direction, e.g. zig-zag.	
	4 Repeat No.3 running.		Move markers 20m apart.
	5 Choose 1 track and travel from 1 marker to the other with a change of speed.	Awareness of change of speed.	
	Jumping		
	1 Choose 1 track, run and jump from 1 marker to the other with a change of speed.	Feet together, arms out for balance. Push hard and bend knees and ankles.	In a space; ropes/hoops could be used for bouncing in different directions.
	2 Practise bouncing for distance/ropes increase distances between ropes.	Jumping & demonstration.	2 ropes per child; child to choose initial distance between ropes.
	3 In-the-river-and-on-the-bank: children stand on either 'bank' of the 'river'. On command 'In the river', children bounce into the river; and on command ' On the bank', children bounce on to either bank.		Ropes/canes end to end and suitable distance apart to mark bank-river-bank.
Concluding activity			

Key Stage 1 • Year 1 • Lesson 6

LEARNING OUTCOMES

1 To walk and run in relays.
2 To bounce in different directions and for height.

Section	Content	Points	Facilities / equipment
Warm-up			
Main activity or challenge	**Walking and running**		
	1 In 2's there-and-back relay over 10m, walking.	Revision of fast walking action. Go round markers. Look behind when walking backwards.	Lines/markers to be used for start and return.
	2 As No.1, but walk forwards to marker and backwards to start.		
	3 There-and-back relay in 2's: walk to marker 1, run to marker 2, walk to marker 3, run back to start.	Awareness of change of speed.	3 markers per couple, 6m apart; each set of markers 2m apart; lines/markers to be used for start.
	4 As No.3, but walk forwards to marker 1, backwards to marker 2, sideways to marker 3.	Awareness of change of direction.	
	5 As No.4, but running.	All relays require you to touch next person before that person starts.	
	Jumping		
	1 Bounce on the spot, then forwards/backwards/sideways.	Feet together, arms out for balance, push hard and bend knees and ankles.	In a space; ropes/hoops could be used for bouncing in different directions.
	2 Bounce for height.		In a space.
	3 In 4's, practise bouncing for height.	Experiment with bouncing forwards, backwards, sideways. Which way is best? Demonstration.	Low obstacles, such as skittles and canes, in a space.
	4 Bouncing circuit for distance, variety and height.	All go round the same way.	Skittles and canes of varying heights; 2 ropes at varying distances apart; hoops, cones, bean bags, etc.
Concluding activity			

Key Stage 1 • Year 1 • Lesson 7

LEARNING OUTCOMES

1 To take part in a running relay.
2 To practise a 2-handed-push throwing action and use it in a competition.

Section	Content	Points	Facilities / equipment
Warm-up			
Main activity or challenge	***Running in relays***		
	1 There-and-back relay in 3's. Run past all cones. Touch last cone and return.	Revision of running action: a) run on balls of feet; b) elbows in.	4 cones per couple, suitably spaced; each set of cones 2m apart; lines/ markers to be used for start.
	2 There-and-back-zig-zag relay in 3's. Run in and out of cones.	Small steps when changing direction.	
	3 There-and-back curved relay in 3's. Run past first 3 cones, round 4th cone and back.	In all relays you must touch next person before that person starts.	
	Throwing: 2-handed-push		
	1 Throw to partner from a) sitting, b) kneeling, c) standing. 3 throws in each position, then change.	Explain and demonstrate: fingers spread and 1 foot in front of other, push from legs/body/shoulders, then wrist and fingers follow through. Choice of apparatus. Correct throwing action. Demonstration.	Balls/bean bags; in a space, 3m apart.
	2 In 2's, practice two-handed throw. Increase distance.	Correct action.	In a space, 3m apart and facing each other, class to form 2 lines.
	3 2-handed throwing competition in 2's. 1 throw and one mark; 3 throws each.	Practise throwing for distance. Children choose apparatus.	Line/markers for throwing point; markers for measuring; ball/bean bags/quoits; each couple 3m apart.
Concluding activity			

Key Stage 1 • Year 1 • Lesson 8

LEARNING OUTCOMES

1 To skip and gallop.
2 To practise catching and the 2-handed-push throwing action.
3 To take part in a skipping relay.

Section	Content	Points	Facilities / equipment
Warm-up			
Main activity or challenge	***Skipping and galloping***		
	1 Skip avoiding others.	Awareness of space & others.	Large defined area marked out with lines or cones.
	2 Teach skipping.	On the spot, hop on 1 foot then hop on the other foot. Keep repeating. Now you are skipping.	
	3 Repeat skip travel.	Action demonstration. Awareness of space & others.	
	4 Gallop avoiding others.	Awareness of space & others.	
	5 Teach galloping.	Take 1 step forwards, bring back foot forwards to side of front foot. Repeat. Now you are galloping.	
	6 Repeat gallop travel.	Action demonstration. Awareness of space & others.	
	7 In 2's follow-my-leader, skipping/galloping.	Action demonstration. Awareness of space & others. Demonstration.	
	Throwing: 2-handed-push		
	1 In 2's, 1 throws to target from a) sitting, b) kneeling, c) standing, and other retrieves.	Revise action: fingers spread, 1 foot in front of other, push from legs/body/shoulders, then wrist and fingers follow through.	Line/marker for throwing point; hoop/skittle for target 3m away; balls/bean bags.
	2 In 2's, 5m apart with hoop between. Throw ball into hoop for partner to catch and return.	How many times can you throw and catch ball before it is dropped?	1 ball/hoop per couple.
	Skipping relay		
	There-and-back skipping relay in 2's (20m).		Lines/markers to be used.
Concluding activity			

Key Stage 1 • Year 1 • Lesson 9

LEARNING OUTCOMES

1 To skip and gallop in competitions.
2 To run and leap for distance.

Section	Content	Points	Facilities / equipment
Warm-up			
Main activity or challenge	**Skipping and galloping**		
	1 Revise skipping and galloping.	Revise action.	In a space.
	2 Skipping races (20/30m).		Lines/markers to be used for start and finish; no lanes.
	3 Galloping races.	Revise action first.	
	4 Skipping/galloping relay in 4's, 2 x 2.	Children have choice of travel. Must touch next person before that person starts.	Lines/markers to be used at each end of relay, 20m apart.
	Jumping		
	1 Leap on the spot: a) 1 foot to other; b) 1 foot to both.	Push hard bending knees and ankles.	Large defined area marked out with either lines or cones.
	2 As above, but step and leap.		
	3 As above, but run and leap.	Demonstration of action first.	
	4 Run and leap over 2 ropes. Increase the distance.		2 ropes per child in a space; child to choose initial distance between ropes.
	5 Leaping circuit. All go same way.	Practise leaping for distance.	Ropes laid out in pairs, varying distances apart.
Concluding activity			

Key Stage 1 • Year 1 • Lesson 10

LEARNING OUTCOMES

1 To vary the speed of running.
2 To run and leap for height.
3 To take part in a jumping circuit.

Section	Content	Points	Facilities / equipment
Warm-up			
Main activity or challenge	***Running for speed***		
	1 Teach running for speed: a) on spot, b) travelling.	Elbows in, arms moving forwards and backwards, increase arm speed; run on balls of feet.	Large defined area marked out with lines or cones.
	2 Children run from teacher and walk back.	Awareness of space/others. Action demonstration.	
	3 As above, but alternate between running slowly and quickly.	Awareness of change of speed. Use whistle.	
	4 Races in small groups over short distances (30/40m).	Running action: look straight ahead and do not slow down.	Lines/markers to be used for start and finish; no lanes.
	Jumping		
	1 Leap for height from a) 1 foot to other, b) 1 foot to both.	Head up, push hard, bend knees and ankles on landing.	Large defined area marked out with lines/cones.
	2 In 4's practise leaping for height: a) with a step/few steps, b) with a run-up.	Action demonstration.	Use of low obstacles, such as skittles and canes.
	3 Jumping circuit: hopping, bouncing and leaping. All go round the same way.	Demonstration. Look for variety, height and distance.	Use selection of apparatus suitably arranged in large defined area.
Concluding activity			

Key Stage 1 • Year 1 • Lesson 11

LEARNING OUTCOMES

1 To practise a standing sprint start.
2 To practise the 1-handed-push throwing action.
3 To take part in a running relay.

Section	Content	Points	Facilities / equipment
Warm-up			
Main activity or challenge	**Standing start running for speed**		
	1 Practise standing start in 2's. Few goes each then change.	Teach standing start. Explain and demonstrate. 1 foot of other, behind line; knees and arms bent; look straight ahead; drive with arms and legs. 1 starts and 1 gives orders: 'On your marks, get set, go'. Action demonstration.	Large defined area marked out with lines or cones; line from which to start; children in a line.
	2 Run for 3 secs. and see how far you can go. Repeat.	'On your marks, set, go'. Use of stopwatch and whistle.	Line from which start; stopwatch; hand-held marker.
	3 In 2's, back to back, facing a cone 10m away. Try and get to cone before whistle.	Use of whistle. Starting and running. Action shown first.	2 cones per couple 2m apart.
	Throwing: 1-handed push		
	Practice throw with bean bag, then see how far you can push it a) sitting, b) kneeling, c) standing. 3 throws in each position.	Explain and demonstrate. Stand sideways, 1 foot in front of other; push hard from legs/body/shoulder. Follow through. Action demonstration.	Line/marker as throwing point, 10 to 15m from children 2m apart in a line. Bean bag and marker per child.
	Relay		
	Touch relay in 4's (10/15m). A and B run towards each other, touch hands then return and touch hands with C and D. C and D do same, then relay is repeated.	Revise action for standing start and running.	Lines/markers at each end.
Concluding activity			

Key Stage 1 • Year 1 • Lesson 12

LEARNING OUTCOMES

1 To practise a standing sprint start and running in lanes.
2 To throw using a 1-handed underarm (bowling action).
3 To take part in running relay.

Section	Content	Points	Facilities / equipment
Warm-up			
Main activity or challenge	*Standing start and running in lanes*		
	1 Revise standing start.	Revise action.	Line/marker from which to start. Children in line; track if possible.
	2 Introduce children into lanes.	Stay in lane and look straight ahead, never around or to side.	
	3 Races in lanes using standing start (40/50m).	Do not slow down.	
	Throwing		
	1 1-handed underarm throw/bowl.	Explain and demonstrate. 1 foot in front of other; take arm back and swing forward, releasing ball, etc., at waist height. Experiment with apparatus.	Balls/bean bags/quoits; in a space.
	2 Underarm throw for distance. Competition in 2's.	Choice of apparatus. 3 throws each. 1 throw and 1 mark.	Line/marker for throwing point and marker for throw; pairs 2m apart in line.
	3 In 2's, underarm throw at target. 1 throw, 1 retrieve.	3 throws each. If all successful, move further away. Choice of apparatus.	Line/marker for throwing point; hoop as target; (children choose initial distance); bean bags/balls/quoits.
	Relay		
	Relay race in 4's. All stand facing same way, 20m apart. A runs to touch B, B runs to touch C, C runs to touch D, D runs to marker.	Revise action for standing start and running.	Line/marker for start; marker for finish.
Concluding activity			

Key Stage 1 • Year 2 • Lesson 1

LEARNING OUTCOMES

1 To walk with speed and direction changes.
2 To hop sequentially in different directions.

Section	Content	Points	Facilities / equipment
Warm-up			
Main activity or challenge	**Walking**		
	1 Walk from cone to cone with a change of speed at each.	Revise walking action. Awareness of others and change of speed.	40 cones scattered in area.
	2 Walk quickly from cone to cone. How many can you pass in 20 secs.	Awareness of others. How many?	
	3 Walk quickly from cone to cone with a change of direction at each.	Awareness of others and changes of direction.	
	4 Choose a starting cone, then a) walk to 3 cones in turn, b) repeat but with change of direction at each cone, c) repeat but walk slowly to first cone and quickly to the rest.	Awareness of others, changes of direction and speed. Make sure no one goes to the same cone as you. Demonstration of task.	
	Jumping		
	1 Revise hopping on spot. Change feet.	Revise hopping action.	In a space.
	2 Make 3 hops forwards, backwards and side to side; then repeat making 2 hops in each direction.	Rhythm and control.	
	3 Make up a sequence of 4 hops using different directions. Do sequence twice.	Rhythm and balance, and awareness of directions.	
	4 Class hopping sequence.	Teacher to choose 1 of the sequences, and class to learn and demonstrate.	
Concluding activity			

Key Stage 1 • Year 2 • Lesson 2

LEARNING OUTCOMES

1 To walk and run with speed and direction changes using 'tracks'.
2 To hop for distance and height in competition.

Section	Content	Points	Facilities / equipment
Warm-up			
Main activity or challenge	**Walking and running**		
	1 Walk from cone to cone following a) straight track, b) curved track, c) zig-zag track.	Revision of action.	3 cones per child, 10m apart; in a space.
	2 Choose 1 trackway. Walk from cone to cone showing change of speed.	Awareness of change of speed.	
	3 Choose another trackway and walk from cone to cone showing change of direction.	Awareness of change of direction.	
	4 Run from cone to cone showing 3 trackways each time.		Move cones 15m apart.
	5 Choose 1 trackway. Run from cone to cone showing a) change of speed, b) change of direction, c) BOTH!	Awareness of change of speed and direction. Demonstration.	
	Jumping		
	1 Revise hopping for a) distance, b) height.	Revise hopping action.	In a space.
	2 Free travel round circuit, hopping.	Practise hopping for height/distance. Choose 1 or 2 examples to show.	Ropes laid out in sets of 2, different distances apart; low obstacles out at varying heights.
	3 Class hopping competition in 2's.	1 mark and 1 jump. 3 turns each. Measure to back of heel.	Take-off line/mark; 2 markers per couple 2m apart; children in a line.
Concluding activity			

Key Stage 1 • Year 2 • Lesson 3

LEARNING OUTCOMES

1 To walk and run in a relay competition.
2 To use the 2-handed-push throwing action in an aiming competition.

Section	Content	Points	Facilities / equipment
Warm-up			
Main activity or challenge	***Walking and running***		
	1 Walk-run-walk-run.	Awareness of others and change of speed.	In a space in a large defined area marked out with either lines or cones.
	2 As No.1 but change direction at each cone.	Awareness of change of direction.	
	3 Relay in 4's. Walk to cone 1, run to cone 2, walk back to cone 3, run to cone 4. From cone 4, run to touch next person.	Rule: you cannot start until you have been touched.	2 lines/markers 20m apart; 4 cones.
	4 Zig-zag relay in 4's. Run in and out of cones.		
	Throwing: 2-handed push		
	1 In 2's, practise throwing to each other. Choice of apparatus.	Revise push action.	Bean bags, quoits ball, etc. In a space, 2m apart.
	2 In 2's, throw ball to each other. After 3 successful throws, increase distance.	Task demonstration.	Class in 2 lines, pairs start 2m apart.
	Throwing: 1-handed push		
	1 Practise with a bean bag, then see how far you can throw.	Revise push action.	Line/marker to throw from; bean bag per child; children in a line, 2m apart.
	2 Aiming competition in 2's, using 1-handed or 2-handed push. Choice of apparatus. 3 throws each. 1 point to 1st hoop, 2 points to 2nd hoop, etc.	Revise push action. Who gained the most points? Whole or part of apparatus must land in hoop.	3 hoops suitably spaced; line/marker to throw from; selection of apparatus; in a space.
Concluding activity			

Key Stage 1 • Year 2 • Lesson 4

LEARNING OUTCOMES

1 To skip and gallop with speed and direction changes.
2 To use the 2-handed-push throwing action in aiming and throwing for distance competition.

Section	Content	Points	Facilities / equipment
Warm-up			
Main activity or challenge	**Skipping and galloping**		
	1 Skip avoiding others, then skip changing direction.	Revision of action.	Large defined area marked out with either lines or cones.
	2 Gallop and change direction.	Revision of action.	
	3 Travel from cone to cone. Alternate between skipping and galloping.	Awareness of others.	Cones scattered about area.
	4 Start at a cone. Skip or gallop forwards to cone 1, backwards to cone 2, sideways to cone 3.	Awareness of others. There should only be 1 person at a cone. Awareness of change of direction.	
	5 As No.4, but alternate speed – slow/fast/slow!	Task demonstration.	
	Throwing: 2-handed push		
	1 In 2's, practise 2-handed throw, 2/3m apart. Choice of apparatus.	Revise action.	In a space, using bean bags/balls/quoits, etc.
	2 In 3's pig-in-the-middle using balls.		In a space; 2 children 4m apart, 1 in middle.
	3 Competition in 3's, throwing for distance using a ball. 1 throws, 1 marks and 1 retrieves. 3 throws each.	Task demonstration.	Line/marker for throw; 1 ball/3 markers per group; groups 2m apart in a line.
	4 In 3's, practise throwing for accuracy into a hoop. Choice of apparatus.	Revise action.	Balls/bean bags, etc.
	5 As No.4 but as a team competition. Choice of apparatus. 3 throws each. 1 point each success.	Add up your team score. Winning team?	Hoops and throwing apparatus. Hoops 2m away in line.
Concluding activity			

LEARNING OUTCOMES

1 To sprint and jog straight and around curves.
2 To bounce sequentially in different directions.
3 To skip and star jump.

Section	Content	Points	Facilities / equipment
Warm-up			
Main activity or challenge	**Sprinting**		
	1 Jog-sprint-jog.	Revise action. Use of whistle. Awareness of others.	Large defined area marked out with either lines or cones.
	2 All stand near teacher. On whistle, sprint away for 5 secs.	Awareness of space and others. Furthest away?	
	3 Round-the-corner, in 4's, clockwise. Teams of 4, each numbered 1 to 4. Teacher in middle calls a number and person with that number sprints round outside of each cone and back to base. 1st back gets a point for the team.		Each team has 4 cones.
	Jumping		
	1 Bounce on spot, then bounce forwards, backwards and sideways.	Revise bouncing action.	In a space.
	2 Make up a sequence of 4 bounces changing direction. Repeat.	Rhythm and control. Demonstration.	
	3 Practise star jumps.	Timing and co-ordination.	
	4 Practise 'skiing'.	Timing and co-ordination.	
	5 Teach skip bouncing.	Turn rope all time. Time jump when rope is on floor.	1 rope per child.
	6 Skipping competition. How many? Class, 1 rope each.		
Concluding activity			

Key Stage 1 • Year 2 • Lesson 6

LEARNING OUTCOMES

1 To practise a standing sprint start and running in lanes.
2 To take part in skipping races.

Section	Content	Points	Facilities / equipment
Warm-up			
Main activity or challenge	*Standing start and sprinting in lanes*		
	1 Practise standing start in 2's. 1 practises and other gives orders! Few turns, then change over.	Revise standing start.	Line/marker from which to start; children all in a line.
	2 As No.1, but with 5 sec. sprint after start.		
	3 Races in lanes (40/50m) with standing start.	Revise main points for running in lanes.	
	Jumping		
	1 Revise and practise skip bouncing.	Revise the action.	In a space; 1 rope per child.
	2 Now try skip running, i.e. from 1 foot to other while turning rope.	Keep rope turning; use medium spaced strides. Awareness of others and space. Demonstration.	
	3 Short races (30m) skip running, in small groups.		Markers for start and finish; children line up between markers; no lanes.
	4 Practise skip bouncing and skip running.		
Concluding activity			

Key Stage 1 • Year 2 • Lesson 7

LEARNING OUTCOMES

1 To experience different ways of starting a race.

2 To use the 1-handed underarm throwing action in throwing for distance competitions.

Section	Content	Points	Facilities / equipment
Warm-up			
Main activity or challenge	*Starting and running for variety*		
	1 In 2's, find as many different ways of starting a race as you can.	Remind children of standing start, and look for variety, e.g. lying, kneeling, sitting. Demonstration.	Large defined area marked out with lines/cones.
	2 In 2's invent a race over 20/30m using a) an unusual start, b) a method of running whilst carrying an object NOT IN THE HANDS.	Variety in starting, then variety and between knees, elbows, under chin, etc.	Lines/markers for start/finish; no lanes; bean bags/balls/quoits/shuttlecocks, etc.
	3 Teacher choose 2/3 of children's races which all then try.		
	Throwing: 1-handed underarm throw/bowl		
	1 In 2's, 2m apart, take turns to throw to partner using a) bean bag, b) quoit, c) ball.	Revise the action first.	In a space; bean bag/ball/quoit per couple.
	2 Use a bean bag and practise throwing for distance.	Task demonstration.	Line/marker for throwing point; marker/bean bag per child; children in line, 2m apart.
	3 Class throwing competition. 3 throws each.		
Concluding activity			

Key Stage 1 • Year 2 • Lesson 8

LEARNING OUTCOMES

1 To run over low obstacles.
2 To use the 1-handed underarm throwing action in throwing for accuracy competitions.
3 To skip run.

Section	Content	Points	Facilities / equipment
Warm-up			
Main activity or challenge	***Running over low obstacles***		
	1 On spot, revise skip running.	Revise the action.	Large defined area marked out with lines/cones.
	2 Travel skip running.	Awareness of others and space.	1 rope per child.
	3 Place rope on floor and run over it.	Compare with skip running.	
	4 Travel round area running over ropes.	Awareness of space and others.	
	Throwing: 1-handed underarm throw/bowl		
	1 In 4's, in a square, 2/3m apart. Throw to each person in the square using a) bean bag, b) quoit, c) small ball, in turn.	Revise action. Look for accuracy of throw. Task demonstration.	
	2 As above, but throw to anyone in the square. Use a ball.		
	3 In 4's, throw for accuracy into a hoop in the middle of square. Start in front of hoop and take 1 step back after each successful throw.	Choice of apparatus. Task demonstration.	Balls/bean bags/quoits, etc; in a space.
	Skip running		
	Practise skip running.	Revise the action. Awareness of space and others.	1 rope per child.
Concluding activity			

Key Stage 1 • Year 2 • Lesson 9

LEARNING OUTCOMES

1 To race over low obstacles.
2 To practise combination jumping for distance.

Section	Content	Points	Facilities / equipment
Warm-up			
Main activity or challenge	***Running over low obstacles***		
	1 Revise running over ropes.	Revise the action.	Large defined area marked out with lines/cones. 1 rope per child.
	2 Run around area over low obstacles.	Awareness of space and others. Try not to knock into obstacles.	Ropes/boxes/bean bags/cones/flower pots/markers/canes on skittles, etc., suitably arranged in area.
	3 Races over low obstacles over short distances of 20/30m.		Lines/markers for start and finish. Obstacles laid out 3m apart in a long line for children to run over.
	Jumping: combination jumping		
	1 a) Hop-hop-jump, b) step-hop-hop, c) hop-step-hop.	Revise the action. Control, rhythm and balance are all required.	In a space.
	2 Choose one of the above combinations and see how far you can jump.		Take-off line/mark plus 1 marker per child; in a space.
	3 Practise combination jumping.	Variety of actions.	In a space.
Concluding activity			

Key Stage 1 • Year 2 • Lesson 10

LEARNING OUTCOMES

1 To run whilst carrying an object.
2 To practise combination jumping for distance.
3 To hop, step and jump.

Section	Content	Points	Facilities / equipment
Warm-up			
Main activity or challenge	***Running and carrying an object***		
	1 Choose an object and run whilst carrying it, then try 2 or 3 other objects.	Which is the easiest way of holding the object? Awareness of space and others.	Large defined area marked out with lines or cones; selection of objects, e.g. bean bags/shuttlecocks/ balls/quoits, etc.
	2 In 2's, A hands object to B and vice-versa.	Choose an object. Which is the best way of handing over and receiving? Experiment.	In a space.
	3 As above, but running from 10m.	Hand-over action – is it safe and secure?	
	4 There-and-back relay in 2's, 20m apart. Each person goes twice.	Pair choose object. Hand-over action. Must go round markers.	Line/markers for start and return; each pair 2m away in a line.
	5 2x2 relay over 20m.	Choose object. Hand-over action. Do not start early in relays. Obey the starting commands.	Lines/markers 20m apart.
	Jumping: combination jumping		
	1 Revise hop-hop-jump.	Revise actions.	In a space.
	2 Teach hop-step-jump from standing. Practise.	All done for length. 'Same to other to both'. Push, bend, rhythm. Land on 2 feet.	
	3 Hop-step-jump competition in 2's. 1 jump and 1 mark.	Task demonstration. Measure to back of heels.	Line/marker for take-off; 1 marker per child.
Concluding activity			

Key Stage 1 • Year 2 • Lesson 11

LEARNING OUTCOMES

1 To work with a partner to carry and pass an object in relays.
2 To use the overarm throwing action.

Section	Content	Points	Facilities / equipment
Warm-up			
Main activity or challenge	**Running and carrying an object in 2's**		
	1 In 2's, revise running and handing over an object with a there-and-back relay over 20m. Each person goes twice.	Pairs choose object. Hand-over and receive actions. Must go round cone in relay.	In a large defined area marked out with lines/cones, using bean bags/quoits/balls/shuttlecocks, etc.
	2 In 4's, work in 2's and decide what you could carry and pass to another pair.	Experiment with different objects. Hand-over action. Explain to the class!	Ropes/hoops/canes, etc.
	3 4x4 shuttle relay over 20m.	Do not start early in relays; wait until the runner passes the object.	Lines/markers, 20m apart, ropes, hoops.
	Throwing: overarm throw		
	1 Teach overarm throw.	1 foot in front of other. Stand sideways on. Lead with elbow – high – shoulder – wrist – hand.	Bean bags/quoits/balls, etc.
	2 Practise overarm throw.	Choice of apparatus.	Line/marker for throwing line; children throw in a line, 2m apart.
	3 In 2's, 3m apart, practise overarm throw using a ball.		In a space.
	4 As above. How many times can you throw the ball to each other without dropping it?		
Concluding activity			

Key Stage 1 • Year 2 • Lesson 12

LEARNING OUTCOMES

1 To use the high-hand baton change-over action.
2 To use the overarm throwing action in an accuracy competition.

Section	Content	Points	Facilities / equipment
Warm-up			
Main activity or challenge	***Running and carrying an object***		
	1 Introduce relay baton.	Explain and demonstrate.	In a space in a large defined area marked out with lines or cones; 1 baton per pair.
	2 In 2's, face each other and experiment with different ways of handing the baton over.	Variety – demonstrate a few different ideas.	
	3 Practise high hand-over in 2's.	Teach high hand-over: person handing over holds baton toward the bottom and high.	
	4 In 2's, practise running a short distance and handing the baton to partner.	Task demonstration.	
	5 4x4 shuttle relay. Refer to previous lesson.		
	Throwing: overarm throw		
	1 Revise throwing with a) bean bag, b) ball.	Revise stance in particular.	Line/marker for throwing point; bean bag/ball per child; children in line 2m apart.
	2 In 2's, 4m apart. Practise throwing to each other.	Task demonstration.	
	3 Teams of 3 throw at targets 3m away. 1st team to knock targets down wins.	6 pieces of chosen apparatus each.	Groups spaced out along line; cones/skittles/wickets/flower pots, etc., for targets; quoits/bean bags/ball, etc, for throwing.
Concluding activity			

The underlying requirements of the PE NC necessarily apply to KS 2 Athletic Activities. Additionally, we read that the End of KS Description for PE states that the majority of pupils should be able to:

...find solutions, sometimes responding imaginatively, to the various challenges that they encounter in the different areas of activity. They practise, improve and refine performance and repeat series of movements they have performed previously, with increasing control and accuracy. They work safely alone, in pairs and in groups and as members of a team. They make simple judgements about their own and others' performance and use this information effectively to improve the accuracy, quality and variety of their own performance. They sustain energetic activity over appropriate periods of time and demonstrate that they understand what is happening to their bodies during exercise. (DFE 1995:11).

Significantly, all KS 2 pupils are required to take part in Athletic Activities, as well as Games, Gymnastic Activities, Dance, Outdoor and Adventurous Activities and Swimming. The Athletic Activities PoS provides guidance on content and teaching approach.

Pupils should be taught:
(a) to develop and refine basic techniques in running, e.g. over short distances, over long distances, over longer distances, in relays; throwing, e.g. for accuracy/distance; jumping, e.g. for height/distance, using a variety of equipment.
(b) to measure, compare and improve their own performance. (DFE 1995:5)

To summarise, as in KS 1 Athletic Activities, there are three main categories of content: running, jumping and throwing. Each category may again be sub-divided into main areas of emphasis from which units of work and lesson plans are devised, but KS 2 components reflect the increasing emphasis placed on skill acquisition and pupils' developing ability to work with others in co-operation and competition.

Running: variety, forwards, backwards, sideways, downhill/uphill, over obstacles, through gaps, straight/curving/angular directions, carrying and passing object(s); all with speed and/or distance changes; working individually, with a partner, or as part of a team.

Jumping: variety, forwards, backwards, sideways, with/without an approach run, over, off obstacles, combination jumping g, leaping, bounding, hopping, skipping; all with speed, direction, distance and height changes; working individually, with a partner, or as part of a team.

Throwing: variety, with/without an approach run or turn, slinging, pushing, pulling/overarm, lobbing, heaving, bowling/underarm and overarm; all with speed, distance, height and accuracy changes; working individually, with a partner, or as part of a team.

The following lesson plans give clear, concise ideas for teaching these running, jumping and throwing activities to KS 2 children, and in so doing enable progression of content to occur within and between lessons throughout the KS. The lesson structure and ideas for warming and concluding activities were outlined in the previous section. They are reproduced here for convenience.

In PE we should always aim to promote pupils' cardiovascular fitness. Therefore, running features in every lesson throughout the KS.

Each lesson has the following structure.

Warming:	5 minutes.
Running activity:	10 minutes.
Main activity:	15 minutes.
Concluding activity:	5 minutes.

The warming represents *gradual* introduction to exercise through which the body temperature is raised, prior to gentle stretching

ch aim to increase pupils' mobility
y, thereby preparing the body to
maximal speed and range of
herefore, start with some gentle
ping, or brisk walking tasks,
….g which pupils move *constantly*. This is
followed by stretching exercises, all carried out
slowly, without jerking or straining, for
example:

(a) move head from front facing to side; side to
front; front to other side, x5
(b) raise shoulders slowly; together x5, then one
shoulder x5, then the other x5
(c) circle arms slowly backwards x5, then
forwards x5; one arm circles x5, then the other
arm
(d) lift arms out to the side of the body and
rotate them inwards/outwards x5
(e) stand astride, feet shoulder width apart; turn
the upper part of the body as far as it will go
then return to be front facing; repeat rotating to
the other side, x5
(f) bend over until the fingers/hands touch the
ground and the arms dangle; stretch up to reach
as far as possible then repeat x5
(g) stand with legs slightly bent, feet together;
slowly reach down to touch the ground then
stand up again, x5.

The concluding activity serves to calm the
pupils down, both physically and mentally,
before they return to the classroom. Obviously
these final tasks must be carried out slowly and
as a whole class activity. Examples include:

(a) standing, rise up on to the toes x3 and walk
away with good posture
(b) lying on the back with all limbs in a naturally
straight position, arms by the sides; gradually
stand and go through (a) above
(c) jogging slowly on the spot, decrease speed
and movement until standing still; do (a) above.

There follows a complete unit of work for
each year of the KS (12 lessons per year).
Progression of difficulty occurs within and
between years and between KS 1 and 2. Whilst
all the tasks included in these plans have been
taught to juniors, the author recognises that
variation exists in the capabilities and aptitudes
between pupils of the same age in different
schools, and that the schools themselves possess
various types and amount of equipment and
differing facilities. It is important, therefore, that
teaching staff use and, if necessary, modify these
lessons to suit their situation and their childrens'
needs.

KEY STAGE 2
LESSON PLANS

Key Stage 2 • Year 3 • Lesson 1

LEARNING OUTCOMES

1 To run with a change of pace.
2 To practise jumping and combination jumping, including the hop, step and jump.

Section	Content	Points	Facilities / equipment
Warm-up			
Main activity or challenge	**Running with a change of pace**		
	1 Walk-fast, walk-jog-run – run fast, then work back down to a walk and stop.	Awareness of change of speed and others. Use of voice/whistle.	Large area; children in a space.
	2 Jog-sprint-jog-sprint.	Increase arm speed for sprinting. Use of voice/whistle.	Children start in a line.
	3 Race. Jog, then on signal sprint to line 30m away.	Use of whistle. Ease up gradually after reaching line.	Lines/markers for start and finish; no lanes; children in a line.
	Jumping		
	1 Revise different ways of jumping.	Q/A for variety of jumps.	
	2 Practise different ways of jumping: a) 1 to same, b) 2 to 2, c) 1 to other, d) 1 to 2.	Revision of actions of jumping for length and height.	Children in a space.
	3 Combination jumps: Hop-hop-jump; hop-step-hop. Find other ways of combining 3 jumps. Choose 1 way and see how far you can jump. Hop-step-jump. Practise.	Revise actions – need control and rhythm. Variety demonstration.	Children in a space.
	4 Hop-step-jump competition in 2's against partner.	3 jumps each. Jump is measured to where heels land.	Line/marker for take-off point; pairs in a line 2m apart; 2 markers per couple.
Concluding activity			

Key Stage 2 • Year 3 • Lesson 2

LEARNING OUTCOMES

1 To sprint 20/30m.
2 To practise standing vertical jumps.

Section	Content	Points	Facilities / equipment
Warm-up			
Main activity or challenge	*Running: effective sprinting*		
	Sprinting over a short distance in 2's.		
	1 On flat feet then on balls of feet.	Discussion with partner then with teacher on the 'best' way to sprint.	Large area; children in a space.
	2 With knees high then with knees comfortable.		
	3 With elbows out then with elbows in.		
	4 Short then tall.		
	5 With head up then with chin on chest.		
	6 In 2's, practise sprinting 20m; 1 sprint, 1 observe.	Discuss action with partner before changing over. Demonstration of an effective sprint action.	Lines/markers for start and finish; no lanes; pairs 2m apart in a line.
	Jumping: standing vertical jump		
	Stand facing wall and stretch to full extent. Mark wall. Sideways, jump to touch wall as high as possible. Height of jump is distance between the 2 points.	Explain and demonstrate. Practise, then class competition. Stretch knees/ankles when springing up; bend knees/ankles on landing. 3 jumps each.	Walk (indoors/out); chalk; measuring tape.
	Sprinting race		
	Sprinting race over 30m.		Lines/markers for start and finish; no lanes; children in a line.
Concluding activity			

Key Stage 2 • Year 3 • Lesson 3

LEARNING OUTCOMES

1 To jog start and sprint 30m.
2 To practise the two-handed push throwing action in accuracy competitions.

Section	Content	Points	Facilities / equipment
Warm-up			
Main activity or challenge	***Running: effective sprinting***		
	1 Revise action from lesson 2, then practise sprinting over short distances.	(See appendix for main points of sprinting)	Large area; children in a space and in a line.
	2 Jog on spot. On signal, move arms backwards/forwards quickly.	Q/A: What happens to legs? Arms?	Children in a space.
	3 Jog-sprint-jog.	Use of whistle. Increase arm speed to sprint.	Children start in a line.
	4 Jog, then on signal sprint to line/marker 30m away.	Use of whistle. Ease up slowly after reaching line.	Lines/markers for start and finish; children in a line to start.
	Throwing: 2-handed push		
	1 In 2's, 2/3m apart. Practise the throw using a ball.	Revise action and demonstrate.	Pairs spaced out along 2 lines; 1 ball per pair.
	2 As above, but increase the distance after 2/3 successful throws.		
	3 In 4's, 2/3m apart and 2 in middle holding a hoop at shoulder height. 6 throws using 2 types of throw, then change over.	Throw the ball through the hoop.	Lines/marker for throwing point; 1 ball and hoop between 4.
	4 As above, but then as a team competition.	Maximum points per couple = 12.	Groups well spaced out.
Concluding activity			

LEARNING OUTCOMES

1 To use a standing sprint start in 50m races.
2 To use the 1-handed overarm and 1-handed underarm throwing actions in distance competitions.

Section	Content	Points	Facilities / equipment
Warm-up			
Main activity or challenge	**Running: sprinting in lanes and standing start**		
	1 In 2's, 1 gives start orders and partner sprints for 5 secs. Starter marks where the sprint finished. Repeat for improvement, then change over.	Revise sprint action. Teacher to time 5/secs. Demonstration. Ease up slowly after sprinting.	In a space in a large area; line or line of markers to start from; 1 marker per pair for distance; stopwatch.
	2 Practise standing start.	Revise main points for standing start. Task demonstration.	Line or line of markers to start from.
	3 Practise standing start in small groups and in lanes.		
	4 50m races in lanes. Small groups.	Revise main points for running in lanes. Q/A session.	
	Throwing: 1-handed underarm/overarm throw		
	1 In 2's, 2/3m apart, practise both throws, using a choice of apparatus.	Revise the actions and demonstrate, especially the stance. Task demonstration.	Balls/bean bags/quoits, etc.; pairs spaced out; class in 2 lines.
	2 As above, but increase distance after 2/3 successful throws.	Q/A: Which throw is best for distance? 1-handed overarm throw. Why?	
	3 In 4's, 2/3m apart and 2 in middle holding a hoop at shoulder height. Choice of apparatus. 6 throws using both types of throw, then change over.	Q/A: Which throw is best for target work? 1-handed underarm throw. Why? More control and the ball can be seen at all times.	Lines/marker for throwing point; balls/bean bags/quoits, etc.; 1 hoop between groups of 4, well spaced out.
	4 As above, but as a team competition.	Maximum points per couple = 12.	
Concluding activity			

Key Stage 2 • Year 3 • Lesson 5

LEARNING OUTCOMES

1 To use a standing sprint start in 50m races.
2 To compete in a standing long jump competition.
3 To use a stopwatch and/or record results.

Section	Content	Points	Facilities / equipment
Warm-up			
Main activity or challenge	*Sprinting in lanes and standing start*		
	1 Practise standing start and short sprint in small groups and in lanes.	Revise the action of a standing start and running in lanes.	Running lanes.
	2 Races over 50m, timed if desired.	Organise group so that children officiate.	Stopwatch and recording materials.
	Jumping: standing long jump		
	1 Practise standing long jump from take-off with 2 feet. Stand behind line/ marker. Bend legs, swing arms, then push. Bend knees/ankles on landing. Jump is measured to where heels land. Try to increase distance.	Explain and demonstrate, particularly position of head. Task demonstration.	Lines/markers for take-off point; children in a line; 1 marker per child for marking distance.
	2 Standing long jump competition in 2's.	A does 2 consecutive jumps, then B does 2 consecutive jumps starting from where A landed. Repeat 3 times. Which couple jumped the furthest?	As above, but 1 marker per couple for marking distance.
Concluding activity			

Key Stage 2 • Year 3 • Lesson 6

LEARNING OUTCOMES

1 To run and long jump.
2 To hop, step and jump and do a standing long jump.
3 To sprint over short distances.

Section	Content	Points	Facilities / equipment
Warm-up			
Main activity or challenge	**Jumping: long jump**		
	1 Run 4 strides and jump, taking off from 1 foot and landing on 2 feet.	Explain and demonstrate: run quickly; drive knee/arms upwards; stretch legs in air; bend knees when landing; land 2 feet together because it's measured to where heels land. Task demonstration.	In a space in large area; long jump pit.
	2 3 groups: Group 1 practise long jump in pit with teacher; Group 2 practise hop-step-jump; Group 3 practise standing long jump.	Group 1: take-off area rather than board; 4-6-8 stride. Group 2: points scored for landing in areas 1, 2, 3; try to remember points for both hop-step-jump and standing long jump. Group 3: standing long jump. Rotate groups and collate points.	Long jump pit; 2 areas marked out close to pit with line/cones; numbered areas suitably spaced out.
	Sprinting		
	How many times can you sprint between the 2 cones in 20 secs?	There-and-back = 1 point. Teacher to time. Q/A on importance of turn. Refer to next lesson.	Children in a space; stopwatch; 2 cones per child, 10m apart.
Concluding activity			

47

Key Stage 2 • Year 3 • Lesson 7

LEARNING OUTCOMES

1 To take part in shuttle races.
2 To practise the 1 and 2-handed push throwing actions.
3 To use stopwatches when timing races.

Section	Content	Points	Facilities / equipment
Warm-up			
Main activity or challenge	*Shuttle running*		
	1 Start at 1st cone. Run to 2nd cone, then back to finish. Repeat.	Refer to previous lesson for Q/A on importance of turning well.	2 cones per child, 10m apart; class in 2 lines.
	2 Practise the turn.	Push hard off turning foot and sprint away.	
	3 Repeat No.1.	Work hard on turning action. Demonstration.	
	4 Practise 6x10m shuttles in lanes.		
	5 6x10m shuttle races, timed if desired.	Organise children to practise timing.	Stopwatches.
	Throwing: 2-handed push		
	1 In 2's, 1 throw and 1 retrieve. Use netball or similar ball.	Revise the action. 9 throws each. Points scored for ball landing in areas 1, 2, 3. Maximum points = 27. Change over. Remember, the distance the ball is thrown is where it lands initially.	Areas marked out as in Lesson 6 for jumping, but suitably spaced out for throwing distance.
	Throwing: 1-handed push		
	2 As for No. 1 (above).	Revise the action and demonstrate using a bean bag or tennis ball.	
	3 As above, but sitting down.	3 throws each. Maximum points = 9.	
Concluding activity			

LEARNING OUTCOMES

1 To take part in skipping races.
2 To compete using the 1-handed push throwing action.

Section	Content	Points	Facilities / equipment
Warm-up			
Main activity or challenge	*Skip running*		
	1 Practise skip running on the spot.	Revise basic action.	Large area, in a space; 1 rope per child.
	2 Practise skip running in small groups over 20/30m.	Task, then demonstration. Awareness of space, especially if skipping in lanes.	Lines/markers for start and finish; children in a line and well spaced out.
	3 Practise racing start. Organisation as for No.2.	Start with rope behind and on the ground.	Lanes.
	4 Skipping races over 50m, in lanes. Timed if desired.	Organise children to time/judge and record.	Lanes; stopwatches and recording materials.
	Throwing: 1-handed push		
	1 Practise 1-handed push with a ball from a) sitting, b) kneeling, c) standing.	For safety, all throw then all retrieve. 3 throws in each position.	1 ball per child (a heavier type ball, e.g. rounders, kwik cricket or hockey); children well spaced out behind line/markers.
	2 Class competition. As No.1 above, standing. In 2's, 1 throw, then 1 mark and retrieve. Person marking/retrieving stands next to person throwing until all have thrown. 3 throws each.	Distance thrown is where the ball lands initially, not where it may roll to!	1 ball and 2 markers per couple.
Concluding activity			

Key Stage 2 • Year 3 • Lesson 9

LEARNING OUTCOMES

1 To take part in relay running.
2 To practise 2 (from 4) different jumping actions.

Section	Content	Points	Facilities / equipment
Warm-up			
Main activity or challenge	*Relay running*		
	1 2x2 straight relay over 20m.	Touch change and do not start too early!	Lines/markers for start and finish. Groups spaced out.
	2 In 4's, there-and-back relay over 20m.	Go round cone at return.	
	3 As above, but pick up a bean bag at return point.		4 bean bags per group placed behind return cone.
	Jumping: 4 groups/4 disciplines		
	Group 1: practise long jump in pit with teacher, and measure if desired; Group 2: standing triple jump (hop-step-jump); Group 3: 4-stride long jump; Group 4: standing long jump.	So that each group experiences 2 disciplines, rotate thus: Gp.1: long jump, then standing t/jump; Gp.2: standing t/jump, then 4-stride l/jump; Gp.3: 4-stride l/jump, then standing l/jump; Gp.4: standing l/jump, then l/jump. Groups 2, 3, 4: points scored for landing in areas 1, 2, 3. Teacher to record points. Remember your groups for next week.	Long jump pit; 3 areas marked out close to pit with lines/markers; numbered areas suitably spaced out for jumping.
Concluding activity			

Key Stage 2 • Year 3 • Lesson 10

LEARNING OUTCOMES

1 To take part in relay running.
2 To practise 2 (from 4) different jumping actions.

Section	Content	Points	Facilities / equipment
Warm-up			
Main activity or challenge	*Relay running with an object*		
	1 In 2's, practise handing baton to each other.	Revise action of handing over/receiving baton.	Large area: in a space; 1 baton per pair.
	2 In 2's, standing at a cone 10m apart. A walks to B and hands B the baton, B then walks to where A started.	Practise handing over/ receiving action.	2 markers/cones 10m apart per pair; class in 2 lines.
	3 As above, but jogging.		
	4 In 2's, 20m apart. As No.3, but running.		Markers/cones moves to 20m apart.
	5 As above, but a race.		
	Jumping		
	Group 1: practise long jump in pit with teacher, and measure if desired; Group 2: standing triple jump (hop-step-jump); Group 3: 4-stride long jump; Group 4: standing long jump.	So that each group experiences two disciples rotate thus: Gp.1: 4-stride l/jump, then standing l/jump; Gp.2: standing l/jump, then long jump; Gp.3: long jump, then standing t/jump; Gp.4: standing t/jump, then 4-stride l/jump. Teacher to collate points.	Long jump pit; 3 areas marked out close to pit with lines/markers; numbered areas suitably spaced out for jumping.
Concluding activity			

Key Stage 2 • Year 3 • Lesson 11

LEARNING OUTCOMES

1 To take part in relay running.
2 To use the overarm throwing action in a competition.

Section	Content	Points	Facilities / equipment
Warm-up			
Main activity or challenge	***Relay running with an object***		
	1 In 2's, 30m apart. Revise running and handing over baton as last week, but now in lanes.	Task demonstration.	Markers for 30m distance; 1 baton per couple.
	2 As above, but in 4's, (2x2).		1 baton between 4.
	3 In 4's, in lanes over 50m (2x2).		Lines/markers; 1 baton between 4.
	4 As above, but races.		
	Throwing: 1-handed overarm throw (pull)		
	1 In 2's, using a bean bag, 1 throw from a) sitting, b) kneeling, c) standing and 1 retrieve.	Revise the action. 3 throws in each position. Points scored for landing in areas 1, 2, 3. Maximum points = 27. Task demonstration.	Areas marked out as in Lesson 6 for jumping, but suitably spaced out for throwing for distance; 1 bean bag per couple.
	2 Practise running then throwing a bean bag.	For safety, all throw, then all retrieve. Remember, stop before throwing – don't go over the line!	1 bean bag per child; children spaced out.
	3 As above, but now a class competition.	3 throws each. For safety, all throw, then all retrieve.	1 bean bag/marker per child.
Concluding activity			

LEARNING OUTCOMES

1 To sprint carrying a variety of objects.
2 To use foam javelins in an overarm throwing action competition.

Section	Content	Points	Facilities / equipment
Warm-up			
Main activity or challenge	***Running for fun***		
	Races over short distances carrying objects (not in hands!) and with different starts!	Refer to Key Stage 1, Year 2, Lesson 7.	
	Throwing: 1-handed overarm throw (pull)		
	Introduce children to foam javelin.		
	1 In 2's, 1 throw from a) sitting, b) kneeling, c) standing, and 1 retrieve.	Experiment with grip and where to hold javelin. Best grip? 3 turns in each position, then change. For safety, all throw then retrieve on teacher's command.	1 javelin per couple.
	2 In 2's, 1 stand and throw and 1 retrieve.	3 turns each. All throw – all retrieve.	
	3 In 2's, 1 run and throw, 1 retrieve.	3 turns each. All throw – all retrieve.	
	4 As above, but class competition.	3 turns each. All throw then all retrieve. Remember, the distance is where the javelin point initially lands!	2 markers per couple.
Concluding activity			

Key Stage 2 • Year 4 • Lesson 1

LEARNING OUTCOMES

1 To practise sprinting and standing starts.
2 To use a standing long jump and standing triple jump in competition.

Section	Content	Points	Facilities / equipment
Warm-up			
Main activity or challenge	*Sprinting and standing starts*		
	1 Jog on spot, moving arms as quickly as possible.	What happens to legs? Revise sprint action.	Large area; in a space.
	2 Jog on spot, then sprint into a space.	Awareness of others and change of speed.	
	3 In 2's, practise standing start and sprints over short distances.	Revise action of the start in a Q/A session. 1 gives orders while partner starts and sprints. Few turns each. Awareness of space/others.	
	4 In 2's, standing start and sprint for 5 secs. Repeat to increase distance.	Teacher signals start and finish with whistle. 1 runs and 1 marks distance.	Line/markers for start; children in a line; 2 markers per couple; stopwatch.
	Jumping: revise standing long jump		
	1 Take-off with 2 feet and practise jump. Try to increase distance. In 2's, take turns.	Q/A on the action, then demonstrate. 1 jump and 1 mark.	Line/markers for take-off point; children in line, 1 marker per child for distance.
	Jumping: revise standing triple jump		
	2 Practise as for No.1 (above).	Q/A on the action, then demonstrate.	
	3 Competition in 2's, choice of jump from above.	3 jumps each; 1 jump and 1 mark.	Recording materials.
Concluding activity			

Key Stage 2 • Year 4 • Lesson 2

LEARNING OUTCOMES

1   To use standing starts in 50m sprint races.
2   To practise standing long jump, long jump and standing triple jump.

Section	Content	Points	Facilities / equipment
Warm-up			
Main activity or challenge	*Sprinting and standing starts*		
	1 Jog on spot, moving arms as quickly as possible.	What happens to legs?	Large area, in a space.
	2 Jog on spot, then sprint into a space.	Awareness of others and change of speed.	
	3 In 2's, standing start, then sprint for 5 secs. Repeat to increase distance.	Teacher signals start and finish with whistle. 1 run and 1 marks distance. Task demonstration.	Line/markers for start, children in line; 2 markers per couple; stopwatch.
	4 Races in small groups over 50m, timed if desired.		In lanes; stopwatch.
	Jumping		
	Revision of: a) standing long jump, b) standing triple jump, c) long jump. Refer to Year 3 Lesson 6 for all activities.	Q/A on main points.	
Concluding activity			

Key Stage 2 • Year 4 • Lesson 3

LEARNING OUTCOMES

1 To practise sustained running.
2 To use flinging and slinging throwing actions in competition.

Section	Content	Points	Facilities / equipment
Warm-up			
Main activity or challenge	**Running – sustained**		
	1 Start at chosen station and run for 3-5 minutes. Count how many stations you pass. REST!	Spread the effort out. Do not run too quickly. Steady breathing.	Short courses using cones as stations. Make it interesting. Stopwatch.
	2 Run between 2 cones for 20 secs. Count the number of runs. a) Repeat for 40 secs, then double the runs; b) Repeat for 60 secs, then triple the runs.	Child to choose distance between cones. Turning action is important. Rest between each shuttle. Teacher to time.	2 cones per child in a space; stopwatch.
	Throwing: 1-handed underarm throw (fling & sling the ring!)		
	1 Practise flinging from a) sitting, b) kneeling, c) standing.	Explain, then demonstrate. Stand sideways with straight arm across body. Wind up. Fling 'through' legs and body. Fling high. For safety, all throw then all retrieve. 3 turns in each position.	Line/markers for throwing point; children spaced out. Use quoits.
	2 Practise slinging a quoit.	Start with arm out to the side of the body. Demonstration.	
	3 Competition: 1 turn each at slinging the quoit and 1 turn at flinging the quoit.	2 throws each! Which type of throw went further? Why?	1 quoit per child. Area as above.
Concluding activity			

56

Key Stage 2 • Year 4 • Lesson 4

LEARNING OUTCOMES

1 To practise sustained running.
2 To use slinging throwing action in competition.

Section	Content	Points	Facilities / equipment
Warm-up			
Main activity or challenge	***Running – sustained***		
	1 Run 100m in exactly 30 secs. Repeat 5 times.	Rest in between runs. Judgement of time, pace and distance. Maintain a consistent effort.	Running track.
	2 In 2's, follow a track and try and arrive back at the first cone at the same time as your partner. Repeat 5 times.	Judgement of pace. Demonstration.	8 cones, 5m apart.
	Throwing: 1-handed throw (sling)		
	1 Practise sling, standing sideways.	(See appendix for main points). Task demonstration. For safety, all throw then all retrieve.	Lines/markers for throwing point; children spaced out; quoits/foam discus.
	2 Class competition: sling it! In 2's, 1 throw and 1 mark. Children marking stand behind throwers and observe spot where apparatus initially lands. Then, when all have thrown and on teacher's command, they place markers. 3 throws each.		2 markers and 1 quoit/ foam discus per pair.
Concluding activity			

Key Stage 2 • Year 4 • Lesson 5

LEARNING OUTCOMES

1 To skip run 5m.
2 To practise standing long jump, long jump and standing triple jump.
3 To practise timing, judging or recording.

Section	Content	Points	Facilities / equipment
Warm-up			
Main activity or challenge	**Skip running**		
	1 Practise skip running a) on the spot, b) on the move.	Revise the action. Awareness of space and others. Demonstration of task.	Large area; in a space; 1 rope per child.
	2 In 2's, there-and-back skip relay.	Do not start too soon! Leave when partner is level with marker.	Lines/markers for start and return, 30m apart; pairs in a line 2m apart; 1 rope per child.
	3 Practise in lanes then races over 50m in small groups, timed if desired.	Organise children to time/judge/record.	Lanes and stopwatches; recording materials.
	Jumping		
	Revision of a) standing long jump, b) standing triple jump, c) long jump. Refer to Year 3 Lesson 9 for all activities.		
Concluding activity			

Key Stage 2 • Year 4 • Lesson 6

LEARNING OUTCOMES

1 To sprint shuttle run.
2 To practise standing long jump, long jump and standing triple jump.

Section	Content	Points	Facilities / equipment
Warm-up			
Main activity or challenge	**Shuttle running**		
	1 Start at cone A. Run to cone B and back to cone A as quickly as possible.	Q/A on turning action.	Large area; in a space; 2 cones per child, 10m apart.
	2 Practise turning when you get to cone B.	Demonstration of the task.	
	3 Repeat No.1.		
	4 Now practise 6x10m shuttles.	Demonstration.	
	5 Races. 6x10m shuttles. Timed if desired.		Lanes if possible.
	Jumping		
	Revision of a) standing long jump, b) standing triple jump, c) long jump. Refer to Year 3 Lesson 9 for all activities.		
Concluding activity			

LEARNING OUTCOMES

1 To sprint in relay races over low obstacles.
2 To practise the heaving throwing action.

Section	Content	Points	Facilities / equipment
Warm-up			
Main activity or challenge	*Running over low obstacles*		
	4 groups.		
	1 Run over obstacles and jog back to group. Repeat 3/4 times.	Establish leading leg.	Line/markers to start; selection of apparatus, i.e. canes on bean bags, canes on skittles, foam or card hurdles at very low height.
	2 Repeat No.1, but try to establish the same number of strides between obstacles.	Establish leading leg. Rhythm.	Suitable space for the same stride pattern.
	3 There-and-back relay race over obstacles.	Touch change. Do not start too soon!	
	Throwing: 2-handed overhead throw (heave)		
	1 In 2's, 3m apart, throw to partner as high as possible, using netball or similar throw.	Explain and demonstrate technique. Back to direction of throw; bend knees; turn body; thrust up with legs and heave with arms; throw over shoulder and follow through.	Quoit looped onto team braid/band; class in 2 lines; pairs spaced out.
	2 As above, but throw for distance and try to increase it.	Practise technique.	
	3 Class competition in 2's, as No.2. Increase distance after each successful throw. Which pair can finish the furthest away?		
Concluding activity			

LEARNING OUTCOMES

1 To sprint in relay races over low obstacles.
2 To practise the heaving throwing action.

Section	Content	Points	Facilities / equipment
Warm-up			
Main activity or challenge	***Running over low obstacles***		
	1 In 3's or 4's, practise standing start and running over 1st hurdle.	Revise action of standing start. Establish number of strides to 1st hurdle and your leading leg. Member of group to give start orders.	Apparatus as last week, lines/markers to start.
	2 Repeat, but now run over 2 hurdles.		
	3 Now over 4 hurdles.	Establish a regular stride pattern if you can.	Move top 2 hurdles so that they are equally spaced from bottom 2 hurdles.
	4 There-and-back relay race over hurdles, then sprint back.	Touch change. Do not start too soon! Do not run back over hurdles.	Top/bottom groups to join together.
	Throwing: 2-handed overhead throw (heave)		
	1 Try a backward throw over the head for partner to catch.	Revise action from last week in a Q/A session.	Class in 2 lines; pairs spaced out; 1 netball per pair.
	2 As No.1, but with quoit. Partner to stand by side then to retrieve.	Teacher demonstration to remind class. Awareness of others. Technique/demonstration.	Line/markers for throwing point; quoit on a braid per pair. Pairs well spaced out.
	3 As above but over shoulder.	Few turns each. All throw, then all retrieve.	
	4 Class competition in 2's. Backward throw overhead (as in No.1).	3 turns each. 1 throw and 1 retrieve for safety.	2 markers per pair.
Concluding activity			

Key Stage 2 • Year 4 • Lesson 9

LEARNING OUTCOMES

1 To use the upsweep change-over action in relay races.
2 To take part in a standing vertical jump competition.

Section	Content	Points	Facilities / equipment
Warm-up			
Main activity or challenge	*Relay running with an object*		
		Teach then demonstrate relay change-over: a) person *handing* baton over; holds baton at end in right hand, then sweeps baton up into partner's hand. b) person *receiving* baton; faces forwards, holding left hand back with fingers and thumb facing downwards, and grips baton firmly.	
	1 In 2's, practise a) walking, b) jogging, c) running.	Practise each twice and rotate so that all practise giving/receiving.	Large area, in a space; 1 baton per pair; 4 cones per group 15m apart in a line for No's. 2/3.
	2 In 3's, practise relay as shown. Last person goes to last cone, a) walking, b) jogging, c) running.		
	3 In 3's, relay race walking, as No.2.		
	Jumping		
	1 Revise standing vertical jump.	Explain and demonstrate.	Wall-indoors/out; chalk.
	2 Standing vertical jump: class competition. 3 jumps each.	Teacher to measure jump.	Chalk and cane/tape measure.
Concluding activity			

LEARNING OUTCOMES

1 To use check marks in a relay competition.
2 To practise high jumping.

Section	Content	Points	Facilities / equipment
Warm-up			
Main activity or challenge	**_Relay running with an object_**		
	1 In 2's, person receiving baton stands at second cone then takes 4 paces towards the first cone and places small marker on ground; return to second cone. Person giving the baton starts 5m back from first cone. When he/she gets to marker, then move from second cone, receive baton and finish at third cone. Try a) walking, b) jogging, c) running. Take a few turns each.	Revise change-over with Q/A session. Person receiving – look round at partner until he/she gets to marker, then face forwards and do not look round again!	3 cones in a line well spaced out + 1 baton per pair.
	2 As above, but in 3's.		4 cones 30m apart in a line.
	Jumping: high jump		
	1 In 4's, cane on lowest level, jump over and repeat to highest level.	Q/A on best way to jump for height: from 1 or 2 feet?	In a space; 2 wire skittles/ 1 cane per group.
	2 Cane on highest level. Start 3/4 strides away and jump a) facing, b) from right side, c) from left side.	Q/A on best angles of approach and why.	
	3 Some groups to change height of cane. All travel round area, jumping over canes.		Some skittles/canes may have to be re-arranged.
Concluding activity			

LEARNING OUTCOMES

1 To use check marks and the upsweep change-over action for sprint relay racing.
2 To take part in a high jumping and a jumping competition.

Section	Content	Points	Facilities / equipment
Warm-up			
Main activity or challenge	***Relay running with an object***		
	Practise in 4's over 50m.	Introduce change-over in lanes. Person *receiving* baton stands on outside of lane, looks at marker for signal to start running, then runs fast and does not look round! Baton is gripped firmly; on approaching partner, without slowing down, sweeps baton UP into partner's hand, releases it and slows down. Do not leave lane until all runners have gone. Explain and demonstrate.	Large space, in lanes; 1 baton per group of 4.
	Jumping: high jump		
	1 Revise No.2 from last week.		In a space; 2 wire skittles/ 1 cane per group.
	2 Showjumping competition in 2's, 1 jumps course for 1 min. while other counts points gained.	Some groups to lower canes. Teacher to give jumps points according to height. Deduct 2 points for dislodged cane. If time, attempt a 2nd round.	'Arena' already arranged from previous activity. Some skittles/canes may have to be re-arranged.
Concluding activity			

Key Stage 2 • Year 4 • Lesson 12

LEARNING OUTCOMES

1 To practise the push and overarm throwing actions.
2 To take part in a sprint relay race (4x50m).

Section	Content	Points	Facilities / equipment
Warm-up			
Main activity or challenge	**Throwing: 1-handed push**		
	1 Practise with a bean bag.	Revision of action. Explain and demonstrate.	Line/markers for throwing point; children spaced out; 1 bean bag per child.
	2 3 throws each. Who can throw the furthest?	For safety, all throw then all retrieve on command.	1 bean bag/1 marker per child.
	Throwing: 1-handed overarm throw/pull		
	1 Practise standing throws.	Revision of technique. Explain and demonstrate. Choice of apparatus. For safety, all throw then all retrieve on command.	Foam javelins/bean bags/small balls; line/markers for throwing point; children spaced out.
	2 Now run and throw. Practise.	For safety, all throw then all retrieve on command. Stop before you go over the throwing point.	
	3 Competition in 2's, 3 throws each. Who can throw the furthest? Standing or running throw.	Choice of apparatus, but both to have same. For safety, all throw then all retrieve on command.	As above, 2 markers per pair.
	Relay races		
	4x50m relay races.		
Concluding activity			

LEARNING OUTCOMES

1 To sprint 75m.
2 To practise high and speed jumping.

Section	Content	Points	Facilities / equipment
Warm-up			
Main activity or challenge	***Running – sprinting over 75m***		
	1 Jog-sprint-jog-walk.	Use of whistle. Awareness of space, others, change of speed.	Large area, in a space.
	2 Start on line. On whistle, sprint and see if you can reach your cone before whistle blows again.	Use of whistle. Which pupil is nearest to his/her cone?	Line/markers to start; 1 cone per child 20m from start; children spaced out.
	3 Start on line. Sprint to cone and gradually slow down.	Explain how to stop gradually after sprint.	
	4 75m races in small groups.	Revision of main points: Track, running in lane etc.	Track.
	Jumping: vertical high jump		
	Practise in 2's. How can you help your partner to improve, e.g. better observation?	Revise action with a Q/A session/ Task and demonstration. Teach children how to measure.	Wall-indoor/out; chalk.
	Jumping: high jump		
	1 In 4's, cane on lowest level. Jump and repeat to highest level.	Q/A on best way to jump for height: take-off from 1 foot or 2?	Groups in space; 2 wire skittles/1 cane per group.
	2 Cane on highest level. Start away and jump a) facing, b) from right side, c) from left side.	Q/A on angles of approach and why? Take-off left is leading leg.	
	3 Some groups to change height of jumps. Travel round and jump as many as you can in 1 min.	1 point for each 'clear' jump. Teacher to time.	Some re-arranging may have to be done. Stopwatch.
Concluding activity			

LEARNING OUTCOMES

1 To use a standing start in sprinting 75m.
2 To practise the scissors high jumping technique.

Section	Content	Points	Facilities / equipment
Warm-up			
Main activity or challenge	*Running – standing start sprinting over 75m*		
	1 Start on a line with a partner. On whistle, see if you can sprint to your cone before your partner and before next whistle.	Use of whistle. Revision of how to stop gradually after sprinting.	Line/markers for start; pairs spaced out in a line; 1 cone 20m from each pair.
	2 Revise standing start. In 2's, take turns to start and sprint.	Task and demonstration. Slow down gradually after sprint.	
	3 75m races, timed if desired.		
	Jumping: high jump/scissors		
	1 In 4's, cane on highest level. Start away from cane, approach; jump. Work in 2's within your group and see how you can help each other improve.	Short approach of 3/5 strides. Note angle of approach; right or left side approach. Push-swing-swing. Work on technique. Demonstration of 1-foot take-off. Is your partner pushing hard enough off ground, swinging legs enough, taking off too close/too far away from cane?	In a space; 2 wire skittles/1 cane per group.
	2 1 turn each over 'proper' high jump.		'Foam' bar and sand pit if available.
Concluding activity			

Key Stage 2 • Year 5 • Lesson 3

LEARNING OUTCOMES

1 To high jump using the scissors technique.
2 To practise vertical jumping.
3 To take part in the jumping circuit.

Section	Content	Points	Facilities / equipment
Warm-up			
Main activity or challenge	*Jumping*		
	3 groups.		
	Group 1 Practise and measure high jump with teacher.	Teach rules: **1** 3 consecutive fails means out. **2** Dislodging bar / passing through plane of upright means a failed jump!	All groups to work in same area.
	Group 2 Standing vertical jump in 2's; 1 jump and 1 measure.	Revise measuring technique.	Wall; chalk; cane; tape measures.
	Group 3 **Show Time!** Take it in turns to complete as many rounds as you can. Work in 2's within group.	1 point for every clear jump; deduct 2 points for any dislodged canes.	Wire skittles and canes arranged at different heights; 8/10 jumps in all.
		Rotate groups. Children to record points and measurements.	
Concluding activity			

Key Stage 2 • Year 5 • Lesson 4

LEARNING OUTCOMES

1 To high jump using the scissors technique.
2 To practise vertical jumping.
3 To take part in the jumping circuit.

Section	Content	Points	Facilities / equipment
Warm-up			
Main activity or challenge	*Jumping*		
	Lesson as for last week. See if you can improve!	Group as for last week but rotate twice.	
Concluding activity			

Key Stage 2 • Year 5 • Lesson 5

LEARNING OUTCOMES

1 To sprint over hurdles.
2 To compete using the 1-handed push throwing action.

Section	Content	Points	Facilities / equipment
Warm-up			
Main activity or challenge	***Running over hurdles***		
	1 In 6's, sprint over hurdles and jog back to group.	Establish leading leg and stride pattern. (See appendix for main hurdling points).	Large area/tracks; lanes/skittles; foam/card hurdles; school hurdles at low height; line to start; 3 hurdles per group.
	2 Work in 2's within groups of 6. 2 turns each at sprinting and taking off as far away from hurdle as possible. Does your partner improve on 2nd turn?	Technique: drive leading foot towards hurdle and lean forwards. Demonstration.	
	3 Races over 3 hurdles. Individual and relays in 6's.		
	Throwing: 1-handed push		
	1 Practise 1-handed push.	Revise action and demonstrate. For safety, all throw then all retrieve on teacher's command.	1 ball per child. Use a heavier small ball (rounders/hockey/kwik cricket ball). Line/markers for throw point. Children spaced out.
	2 Class competition in 2's: 1 throw and 1 retrieve/mark.	Marker to stand well away from thrower and only mark/retrieve when all have thrown. Choice of ball. Remember, the ball is marked where it lands initially!	Throwing line and markers/retrievers 15m away from throwers. 1 ball/2 markers per pair.
Concluding activity			

LEARNING OUTCOMES

1 To sprint over 35m hurdles.
2 To compete using the overarm throwing action.

Section	Content	Points	Facilities / equipment
Warm-up			
Main activity or challenge	***Running over hurdles***		
	Repeat No's 1 and 2 from last week		
	3 In 2's, practise fast standing starts away from hurdles. Few turns each. What could your partner do to improve his/her start?	Revise technique.	
	4 Races over 35m, timed if desired.	Technique demonstration.	3 lanes; 6 hurdles/lanes suitably spaced.
	Throwing: 1-handed overarm throw		
	Introduce rounders ball throw.	Revise action and demonstrate.	
	1 In 2's, 1 throw and 1 retrieve.	For safety, all throw, then retrievers get balls. Retrievers to stand with throwers until all have thrown.	Large area; 1 rounders ball; 2 lines/markers for throw point. Children well spaced out.
	2 Competition – 3 throws each using a bean bag.	For safety, all throw then all retrieve on teacher's command.	1 bean bag per child.
Concluding activity			

Key Stage 2 • Year 5 • Lesson 7

LEARNING OUTCOMES

1 To practise sustained running.
2 To practise the overarm, 1 and 2-handed push throwing actions.

Section	Content	Points	Facilities / equipment
Warm-up			
Main activity or challenge	**Sustained running**		
	1 In 2's, follow a track and try to arrive back at 1st cone at same time as your partner. 1 person to change pace and other to keep up.	Judgement of pace.	8 cones 5m apart.
	2 Start at a station. Run for 3 mins. and see how many stations you can pass.	Spread the effort out. Steady breathing. Do not run too quickly.	Short, interesting course using cones as stations and ropes as guidelines. Stopwatch.
	Throwing		
	3 Groups: Group 1-practise and measure rounders ball throw with teacher; Group 2-1-handed push; Group 3-2-handed push.	Groups 2/3 have choice of apparatus. Points awarded for landing in areas 1, 2, 3. Remember your points and record them. Work in 2's so 1 can retrieve. Remember your groups for next lesson.	All groups spaced out in large area. Lines/markers are suitably spaced for throwing; balls/bean bags/quoits, etc; recording materials.
Concluding activity			

Key Stage 2 • Year 5 • Lesson 8

LEARNING OUTCOMES

1 To walk/run 800m.
2 To practise (from) the overarm, 1-handed and 2-handed push throwing actions.
3 To time/judge the 800m.

Section	Content	Points	Facilities / equipment
Warm-up			
Main activity or challenge	*Sustained running over 800m*		
	In 2's, over 800m, choose a) walking and jogging or b) jogging and running. 1 to change pace at different times and other to keep up. Change over.	Steady breathing and spread the effort out.	Track or appropriate course.
	Throwing		
	Groups as for last week, but rotate twice.		
Concluding activity			

LEARNING OUTCOMES

1 To run 800m.
2 To practise (from) the standing long jump, standing triple jump and long jump.
3 To measure and record long jumps.

Section	Content	Points	Facilities / equipment
Warm-up			
Main activity or challenge	*Running over 800m*		
	Divide up into 2 groups. Pupils have a choice of a) jogging and running or b) running over 800m. Runners timed if desired.	Steady breathing and spread the effort out.	Track or similar.
	Jumping		
	Get into 3 groups. Refer to Year 3 Lesson 6 for details. Practise all 3 disciplines with teacher. Have a few turns each.	Revise technique of standing long jump, standing triple jump and long jump. Explain and demonstrate. Children record their points for standing triple jump and measure and record standing long jump. Remember groups for next week.	Tape measure and recording materials.
Concluding activity			

LEARNING OUTCOMES

1 To revise relay check marks and change-overs.
2 To practise (from) the standing long jump, standing triple jump and long jump.
3 To measure and record long jumps.

Section	Content	Points	Facilities / equipment
Warm-up			
Main activity or challenge	**Relay running with an object**		
	1 In 2's, 2 cones 3m apart; 1 child at each cone, both facing same direction. Both leave cones at same time, and A hands baton to B while a) walking, b) jogging.	Revise change-over. Q/A on action. Demonstration.	In a space; class in 2 lines; 2 cones per pair.
	2 In 2's, 2 cones 20m apart, B stands at cone, takes 4 paces back, places marker on floor, then returns to cone. A stands at other cone with baton. Both face same direction. A runs to hand baton over and B runs way to receive it when A reaches marker.	Task demonstration.	
	Jumping		
	As last week, but rotate groups as follows: Group 1-standing triple jump, then standing long jump; Group 2-standing long jump, then long jump; Group 3-long jump, then standing triple jump.	Results for standing long jump and standing triple jump measured and record by children, collated by teachers. Who got the highest points? Who improved from last week?	Tape measure and recording materials.
Concluding activity			

Key Stage 2 • Year 5 • Lesson 11

LEARNING OUTCOMES

1 To practise the downpass relay change-over action.
2 To take part in a 4x50m sprint relay.
3 To practise flinging and slinging throwing actions.

Section	Content	Points	Facilities / equipment
Warm-up			
Main activity or challenge	*Relay running with an object*		
	1 In 2's, practise downpass change-over in lanes. Few turns each, then change over.	Revise action of relay change-over in lanes. Task demonstration.	Track; 1 baton per pair.
	2 Relay races, 4x50m.		
	Throwing: 1-handed underarm throw (sling it or fling it!)		
	1 In 2's, with a comfortable grip, fling the hoop to partner for partner to catch.	Revise fling action.	1 small hoop per pair; class in 2 lines; pairs well spaced.
	2 Now try slinging it!	Revise sling action.	Use quoit/foam discus if no small hoops available.
	3 In 2's, choose 1 of the throws and choose apparatus. Stand back, turn a complete rotation, and fling/sling apparatus to partner to catch.	4 turns each and 4 points for each successful catch.	Class in 2 lines and very well spaced out; choice of apparatus.
	Hoop la!		
	In 2's, side by side, 1 person holding hoop. Roll hoop, and partner runs alongside and attempts to run through hoop before it collapses. How many times can you do it?		1 hoop per pair.
Concluding activity			

LEARNING OUTCOMES

1 To work as part of a team in a running competition.
2 To practise the standing heave throwing action.

Section	Content	Points	Facilities / equipment
Warm-up			
Main activity or challenge	**Team running**		
	1 In 6's, jog within area. When the teacher calls out a number, rush to form groups of that number.	Avoid all other runners and run quietly. Listen!	Large, flat area.
	2 *Make the Cake* Team competition in 6's. On signal, each team tries to win by running together to the teacher and correctly reciting all 6 ingredients.	Before running, team decides strategy, i.e. who runs to which cone and where they meet to collate answers.	7 cones spaced out over large area. Under 6 cones is a name of a cake ingredient.
	Throwing		
	Heave (2-handed throw). 1 In 2's, practise standing and throwing quoit backwards over head. 2 Start with back to direction of throw; turn and heave quoit over shoulder. 3 As No.2, but rotate quoit once around head before throwing. 4 As No.3, but rotate quoit twice around head before throwing!	(See Appendix for main points).	1 quoit (tied onto a braid band) per pair, all behind throwing line waiting teacher's commands.
Concluding activity			

Key Stage 2 • Year 6 • Lesson 1

LEARNING OUTCOMES

1 To practise standing start and sprinting.
2 To sprint 75m.
3 To perform and measure long jumps.
4 To practise standing triple jumps.

Section	Content	Points	Facilities / equipment
Warm-up			
Main activity or challenge	**Sprinting over 75m**		
	1 Start behind the line. On teacher's whistle, run as far as possible in 6 secs. Repeat. 2 75m races in small groups.	Revise standing start and sprint action. Remember stop gradually after sprinting.	Large area, preferably track with lanes.
	Jumping		
	1 Practise each of jumping techniques learnt previously (see Year 5 Lessons 9 & 10). 2 3 groups: Group 1-long jump and measuring with the teacher; Group 2-standing triple jump; Group 3-standing long jump.	(For these basic actions, see Appendix). Groups 2/3 record and give their points to teacher at end of lesson.	Flat, grassy area; measuring and recording materials. Refer to Year 3 Lesson 6 for group organisation.
Concluding activity			

Key Stage 2 • Year 6 • Lesson 2

LEARNING OUTCOMES

1 To compete a timed 75m sprint.
2 To practise standing starts.
3 To perform and measure long jumps.
4 To practise standing triple jumps.
5 To time and/or record 75m sprints.

Section	Content	Points	Facilities / equipment
Warm-up			
Main activity or challenge	*Sprinting over 75m*		
	1 Revise standing start.	(See Appendix for main points of standing start). Remember, stop gradually after sprinting. Rotate groups so that children time and record.	Flat, grassy area; track if possible; stopwatches; recording materials.
	2 In 2's, on teacher's command, practise racing over 10m using standing start.		
	3 Timed 75m races.		
	Jumping		
	As for Year 6 Lesson 1, but groups rotate to 2nd activity.		
Concluding activity			

Key Stage 2 • Year 6 • Lesson 3

LEARNING OUTCOMES

1 To learn how to pace for sustained running.
2 To encourage and support a partner.
3 To jog 800m.
4 To perform and measure long jumps.
5 To practise standing triple jumps.

Section	Content	Points	Facilities / equipment
Warm-up			
Main activity or challenge	**Sustained running**		
	1 In 2's, run together over 2 laps of the trail. Take turns to guess partner's 'secret' topic.	Keep in step with each other and keep talking! Change over if you guess the topic.	Markers to lay trail of 2 laps of 200m each.
	2 Individually, 1 jogs 2 laps of the trail. Partner joins in for the next 2 laps. Run together.	An 800m jog, maintain steady pace.	Use trail, or track.
	Jumping		
	As for Year 6 Lesson 1, but groups rotate to 3rd activity.		
Concluding activity			

Key Stage 2 • Year 6 • Lesson 4

LEARNING OUTCOMES

1 To learn how to pace for sustained running.
2 To encourage and support a partner.
3 To jog 800m.
4 To practise a standing overarm throw.
5 To act responsibly by obeying the teacher's retrieval instructions.

Section	Content	Points	Facilities / equipment
Warm-up			
Main activity or challenge	*Sustained running over 800m*		
	In 2's, run a steady pace together for 1 lap of trail (200m); A continues jogging (B stops) for 2 more laps; B joins in for the last lap. Change over.	Each pupil takes turns to be 'helper' and 'athlete'. Maintain steady pace throughout.	Use trail or track.
	Throwing: rounders ball throw		
	In 2's, 1 throws and 1 retrieves. After each throw and on teacher's command, retrievers run to mark where ball landed. 3 throws each.	(See Appendix for overarm throwing action). Collate points. Did you score more points than your partner? How many children improved their distances?	Place markers to show areas; each area is worth '?' points: ? 'you decide'.
Concluding activity			

Key Stage 2 • Year 6 • Lesson 5

LEARNING OUTCOMES

1 To complete a timed 800m run unassisted.
2 To time, judge, record the 800m results.
3 To practise a standing overarm throw.
4 To act responsibly by obeying the teacher's retrieval instructions.

Section	Content	Points	Facilities / equipment
Warm-up			
Main activity or challenge	*Sustained running over 800m*		
	Each pupil to complete an individual timed run over 800m. (It is NOT a race against one another).	Reminder of need to pace oneself for most of run (practised in 2 previous lessons), though speed can be increased over last 100m. Rotate groups so all experience timing/judging and recording.	Trail or track. Use tape measure to make sure distance per lap same in 2 previous lessons; stopwatch and recording material.
	Throwing: rounders ball throw		
	In 2's, 1 throws, 1 retrieves.	(See Appendix for overarm throwing action). Collate points. Did you score more points than your partner? How many children improved their distances?	Place markers to show areas; each area is worth '?' points: ? 'you decide'.
Concluding activity			

Key Stage 2 • Year 6 • Lesson 6

LEARNING OUTCOMES

1 To practise the hurdling action.
2 To assist a partner.
3 To practise the standing start and starting commands.
4 To practise the scissors jumping action.

Section	Content	Points	Facilities / equipment
Warm-up			
Main activity or challenge	***Running over hurdles***		
	1 Practise sprinting over hurdles and jogging back (down the side). Groups of 6.	(See Appendix for hurdling action). 1 stands by a hurdle to see if hurdler takes off further away on 2nd turn. Take turns to start each other using commands: 'on your marks, get set, go!'	Canes/skittles or foam/card hurdles; 3/4 hurdles per group. If possible, use track lanes. Pupils place hurdles where they wish, up to 25m apart (i.e. each group has its own spacing).
	2 In 2's, 2 turns each at taking off as far away from each hurdle as possible. Sprint!		
	3 Using a standing start, practise sprinting over the hurdles.		
	High jumping		
	1 Practise scissors.	Revision of Year 5 Lesson 2. (See Appendix for scissors jump action).	2 wire skittles and 1 cane per group of 4. Raise cane each time height is cleared.
	2 Practise alternate jumps from right/left side approach.		
Concluding activity			

Key Stage 2 • Year 6 • Lesson 7

LEARNING OUTCOMES

1 To sprint 25m and 40m hurdles.
2 To contribute to group decision making.
3 To practise the standing vertical jump or
4 the scissors or
5 the jumping course.

Section	Content	Points	Facilities / equipment
Warm-up			
Main activity or challenge	*Running over hurdles*		
	1 In 6's (as in Lesson 6), sprint over hurdles so that you take-off on same leg each time.	Using standing start, take turns to practise. Each group to agree spacing for their hurdles.	Each run over 25m, 3/4 hurdles per group.
	2 Repeat No.1.		Increase distance of run to 40m; 6 cane/skittle hurdles and/or low school hurdles per group.
	High jumping		
	Repeat Lesson 3 Year 5. Each group stays on 1 activity.		Sand pit if possible for landing area.
Concluding activity			

Key Stage 2 • Year 6 • Lesson 8

LEARNING OUTCOMES

1 To sprint 40m and 55m hurdles.
2 To contribute to group decision making.
3 To practise the standing vertical jump or
4 the scissors or
5 the jumping course.

Section	Content	Points	Facilities / equipment
Warm-up			
Main activity or challenge	*Running over hurdles*		
	1 In 6's, take turns to use standing start and sprint over 6 hurdles.	(See Appendix for hurdling action).	If possible, 8 hurdles per group of 6, 40m apart.
	2 Take turns to use standing start and sprint over 8 hurdles.		Increase distance to 55m.
	High jumping		
	Repeat Year 5 Lesson 3. Each group tries 2 activities.		If possible, use sand pit when practising scissors.
Concluding activity			

Key Stage 2 • Year 6 • Lesson 9

LEARNING OUTCOMES

1 To revise the upsweep relay change-over action.
2 To incorporate (1) in a 4x50m relay race.
3 To practise the standing heave throwing action.

Section	Content	Points	Facilities / equipment
Warm-up			
Main activity or challenge	*Sprint relay running*		
	1 In 2's, both to be running in same direction when baton is passed.	Revise change-over (see Year 5 Lesson 10).	1 baton/marker per pair; class in 2 lines working from cones 20m apart.
	2 Relay races, 4x50m.	Each pupil works out check mark before 1st race.	1 marker for 3 of 4 runners; 1 baton per team.
	Throwing: heave		
	1 Start with quoit on ground and your back to the direction of throw; heave it over your head.	Feet shoulder width apart, knees slightly bent. Grasp braid with hands close together; swing arms vigorously upwards and backwards. (See Appendix for heaving action, and Year 5 Lesson 12).	1 quoit/braid per pair; pairs well spaced out behind throwing line and retrieve on command.
	2 Repeat stance, but heave quoit over shoulder.		
	3 Repeat stance, but 1st rotate quoit once around head.		
Concluding activity			

LEARNING OUTCOMES

1 To practise the upsweep and downpass relay change-over.
2 To incorporate the downpass action in a 4x50m relay race.
3 To practise the standing sling throwing action.

Section	Content	Points	Facilities / equipment
Warm-up			
Main activity or challenge	***Sprint relay running 4x50m***		
	1 In 2's, both to be running in same direction when baton is passed.	Revise change-over (see Year 5 Lesson 10). See Appendix for main points).	1 baton/marker per pair. Class in 2 lines, working from cones 20m apart.
	2 In above pairs, practise downpass change-over.		
	3 Repeat No.1, with No.2 included.		
	4 Relay races – 4x50m.	Each pupil works out check mark before 1st race.	1 marker for 3 of 4 runners and 1 baton per team.
	Throwing: sling		
	1 In 2's, practise standing slinging action, 3 throws each.	(See Year 5 Lesson 11 and Appendix for the main points). Q/A: How many catches?	Small hoop per pair.
	2 Rotate once before slinging.		
Concluding activity			

Key Stage 2 • Year 6 • Lesson 11

LEARNING OUTCOMES

1 To work as part of a team to maintain sustained pacing.
2 To take part in a team competition over 400m.
3 To practise the pull throwing action, standing and with a short approach run.

Section	Content	Points	Facilities / equipment
Warm-up			
Main activity or challenge	**_Team running_**		
	1 In 4's, jog together for 1 lap of trail.	Run at steady pace which all group can sustain.	Trail of at least 400m per 'lap'.
	2 Race against other teams for 1 lap. Teams MUST each cross the finishing line holding hands.	Before start, each team works out how to maximise chances of winning; i.e. who wants to run alone/together. After race 1, teams discuss result and change/retain plan.	
	3 Repeat.	Discuss result and explain best part of plan to the class.	
	Throwing: pull 1-handed overarm throw		
	1 Practise standing throwing action.	(See Appendix for an explanation of the main points).	If possible, foam/Junior javelins, otherwise size 3 playballs; hoops, all behind throwing line and obey teacher's commands.
	2 Practise throw after a run up of a few strides.		
	3 Using No.1 and/or No.2, have 2 throws each at getting javelin in hoops scattered in throwing area.		
Concluding activity			

LEARNING OUTCOMES

1 To work as part of a team to maintain sustained pacing.
2 To take part in a team competition over 400m.
3 To practise the standing push throwing action.

Section	Content	Points	Facilities / equipment
Warm-up			
Main activity or challenge	*Team running*		
	1 In teams of 5 (mixed ability), jog together for 1 lap (400m).	Maintain pace which all can sustain, Talk about a chosen topic as they run.	A track if possible, with 1 lane per team, making it easier to judge stage distances.
	2 Team competition; each runner completes a part of 1 lap. Winning team has No.5 runner crossing finishing line 1st.	Before racing each team must decide order of runners (i.e. 1st, 2nd, etc.) and how far each will run (at least 80m).	
	3 Repeat No.2.	Discuss result in teams and re-allocate stage distances/order if desired.	
	Throwing: push (1-handed throw)		
	Take turns to push ball as far as possible. 3 goes each. Which pair achieved the most points?	(See Appendix for main points).	Heavy, small ball per pair; in marked area.
Concluding activity			

CROSS-CURRICULAR LINKS AND ASSESSMENT

Cross-curricular links

As with all subjects in the NC, PE contributes to the all-round development of the child. Games and Athletic Activities, with their emphasis on challenges in running, jumping and throwing in individual, pair and team competitions, play a significant part in promoting that development.

Personal and social education

We have already highlighted the importance which is placed on this aspect of a child's development in PE (see pp. 10 and 12). In promoting 'positive attitudes' children are trained in Games and Athletic Activities to obey and recognise the need for rules, and to implement them fairly and consistently and in so doing to take part in honest competition within the conventions of fair play. Therefore, from an early age they should experience estimating, judging and 'measuring' performances.

Many tasks involve the use of apparatus and equipment which, if not used sensibly, could cause injury and/or disruption. In ensuring safe practice, therefore, staff should train children to listen and respond to the teacher's and, if required, their partner's instructions. They also need to learn how to retrieve apparatus safely, for example to collect a thrown projectile and *carry* it back to the throwing line – not *throw* it.

Participation in Games and Athletic Activities necessarily trains children to learn to cope with success and limitations in performance. Individual differences become more apparent as they grow older and with it the need to work in mixed ability groups tolerantly and supportively, particularly towards the gifted and least able. This is very important in tasks which require older junior children to plan a strategy before responding, or to meet to discuss the outcome of that strategy – all relevant in the achievement of the AT (planning, performing and evaluating).

Training children to observe and describe movements is central to the development of a physically educated person. Demonstration of tasks is a key strategy in the promotion of observation and one which is frequently used by teachers. Consequently 'demonstration' features in most of the lesson plans in this book and its use is described in the Appendix.

Communication

This is, of course, vital in training children to work together. There are many examples in Athletic Activities lessons where pupils need to communicate verbally with at least one other child in order to respond to tasks set. This could include assisting each other in the improvement of performance; calling out race times; describing actions; explaining why a particular action is a 'good' choice, and so on. Staff should endeavour to include varying situations in which *all* children are encouraged to communicate constructively and sensibly, and in so doing assist in the promotion of learning and social well-being.

Numeracy

Obviously, the use of objective outcomes (such as 'the number of bean-bags which landed in the hoop'; the metric 'measurement of a vertical jump'; the counting of 'laps completed') in Athletic Activities lessons, lend themselves well to the development of children's numeracy capabilities. Some of this work could link directly with their Mathematics lessons.

Therefore, a combination of classroom work and a growing familiarity with the use of numbers during Athletic Activities lessons could enable children to employ multiplication, addition and subtraction methods, eventually progressing to working out averages and fractions.

Assessment and recording

Assessment of pupil performance is an integral part of the delivery of the NC. The nature of PE is such that, in the main, pupils' responses are fleeting and usually require their colleagues and teachers to look in order to *see* what happens. The transient nature of physical activity, therefore, promotes keen observational powers in teaching staff and children, particularly as

the assessment of pupil performance is formative and summative. By implication, therefore, children from an early age should be encouraged to record their performances. For example: 'the time', 'the distance', 'the number of…'. The teacher can record on a class list pupil achievements according to the relevant criteria or headings.

Running

Upsweep relay changeover. The outgoing runner's (left) hand is held back with the fingers together and thumb facing downwards. The incoming runner's (right) hand holds the end of the baton and lifts it into the next runner's hand. Their hands should *touch*.

Downpass relay changeover. The outgoing runner's (left) arm is held out straight behind them, with the palm uppermost, with fingers together and thumb straight in a 'V' shape. The incoming runner's (right) hand holds the end of the baton and brings it down on to the palm of the next runner.

Hurdling. When you are one step away from the hurdle, lift the leading leg bent and bend the take-off leg so that you drive low at the hurdle. (Remember – it is a running action, not a jumping action.) Reach forward over the hurdle, i.e. right foot and left arm or left foot and right arm, and straighten the leading leg. On landing, get quickly back into your running action.

Sprinting. Run on the balls of your feet with a high knee lift and a vigorous forwards/backwards arm action (not across the body).

Standing start. Start with one foot up to the line, bend the legs and arms and on 'Go', push forwards with the legs, look ahead, and run fast.

Jumping

High jump – scissors. Decide which foot you will take off from (it will be the one further from the bar) and swing the other leg (nearer to the bar) over the bar. Bend forwards as you jump. Land on your feet.

Standing long jump. Start with feet shoulder width apart and crouch down, swing your arms forwards, and push hard from your feet. Look ahead. Land on your toes, feet together, and fall forwards.

Standing triple jump. Decide which foot you will take off from: place this foot up to the line. Hop forwards on to the same foot; skip forwards on to the other foot and jump forwards on to both feet; fall forwards. 'Same, other, both' encourages you to get the correct order.

Standing vertical jump. Stand sideways by a wall and reach up with the nearer arm and mark the wall at the highest point. With the feet together, bend your knees, spring up and mark the wall at the highest point you can reach with the outstretched arm. If marking is difficult, they could, for example, count the number of bricks between the two points.

Running long and triple jumps. Make a 4–6 stride run. The take-off foot should land on the line. Follow the explanation for **standing long jump**.

Throwing

Fling. (This is frisbee throwing.) Hold the small hoop, or quoit, in the dominant hand, in front of your chest with the arm across the body. Extend the arm upwards and forwards and release the hoop at an angle of 45 degrees.

Heave. (This is the early stage of the hammer throwing action.) Start with your back towards the direction of throw and place one foot in front of the other. Right-handed throwers should place the right foot ahead of their left. Hold the band in two hands and turn your body to the left, pulling the quoit over your left shoulder. Aim for a 45-degree angle of release.

Overarm throw. (This is the pull throwing action used for javelin.) Right-handed throwers start standing sideways with their left foot forwards and holding the ball behind them, grasping it in the fingers. Hold the ball behind the body and above the shoulder. Lean back: 'Bend your arm, turn your body and throw the ball.' Finish with your weight forwards on your front foot.

Push (two-handed). (This is similar to the shot putt action.) Start facing the throwing direction with one foot in front of the other. Hold the ball with two hands in front of the chest. Transfer your weight on to the front foot and simultaneously extend the arms and push the ball away with the fingers.

Sling. (This is the throwing action for the discus.) Start sideways-on to the direction of throw, feet shoulder width apart. Hold the quoit in the right hand with the palm facing downwards. Twist the body round and back, then untwist and release the quoit at an angle of 45 degrees in front of the body.

Underarm throw. (This is the underarm bowling action used in rounders.) Start with the left foot in front. Hold the ball as for the overarm throw. Bring the right arm backwards, then transfer the weight on to the front foot and swing the arm forwards, releasing the ball at waist height.

Demonstration

Demonstrations can be made by teacher or pupil. With pupil demonstrations, make sure the child knows what they are going to demonstrate and when, ahead of time. Before the demonstration starts give the class three points to look for. Remember to thank the pupil(s). Never use pupils to show bad examples.

When the teacher demonstrates, give the class three points to look for before starting.

An effective demonstration saves a good deal of explanation and is easily understood and remembered by the children.

INDEX